Fund Your Family's Future

Dario Chin

DEDICATION

For my family, A, Z and B. You are my world and I love you.

CONTENTS

DISCLAIMER

This book is provided for information only and does not constitute, and should not be construed as, investment advice or a recommendation to buy, sell, or otherwise transact in any investment including any products or services or an invitation, offer or solicitation to engage in any investment activity.

The information in this book is provided solely on the basis that you will make your own investment decisions and I do not take account of any reader's investment objectives, particular needs, or financial situation. In addition, nothing in this book shall, or is intended to, constitute financial, legal, accounting or tax advice.

Unlike cash, stock-market based investments aren't guaranteed and can fall in value as well as rise and you could get back less than you invested. Past performance does not guarantee future performance and the value of investments can fall as well as rise. No investment strategy is without risk and markets influence investment performance. Investment markets and conditions can change quickly. Strategies or products can lose money as well as gain. All investors should consider investing only if they can accept the risks associated with investing including a loss of invested capital. No investor should invest without a thorough reading of the risk factors associated with each investment strategy in official documentation provided by the investment provider. Investors with questions should additionally seek independent investment advice tailored to their needs, circumstances, and risk tolerances.

I have taken reasonable care to ensure that the information in this book is accurate, current, complete, fit for its intended purpose and compliant with applicable law and regulation as at the date of issue. No warranty or representation of any kind regarding the accuracy, validity or completeness of the information in this book is given and, to the extent permitted by applicable laws, no liability is accepted for the accuracy or completeness of such information. Any person who acts upon, or changes his or her investment position in reliance on information contained in this book, does so entirely at his or her own risk.

1 INTRODUCTION

I'm in the process of revolutionising my family's wealth – and I want to share my journey with you. There's a financial revolution happening and this book will give you the tools to get involved. Saving money is dead. Interest rates in the UK are terrible, and savers aren't getting rewarded for keeping their hard-earned money in low-interest bank accounts for the big banks to just lend out to someone else. Rising life expectancy in the general population mean millions of people face big reductions in their income when they retire and wage growth for UK workers over the last 10 years has been the lowest since records began in 1949. Health care burdens in old age will be a real problem for a lot of people, property prices are increasing and university fees are the highest they've ever been.

The only way to secure your family's financial future is to invest your money. To make your money work for you. Society is changing and you need to be prepared. Apart from a major political upheaval, the only thing that makes you resilient to these things is a solid financial foundation for you and your family.

This book is challenging the status quo. I'll show you why there has never been a better time to become a DIY investor and why you don't need to be an expert – or pay an expert – to build your family's wealth. The internet has made investing easier than ever before and offers access to the same information for free that was only once accessible to the elite or financial professionals.

Forewarning, this book is biased – it contains much of my own opinion and experience. It gives you examples and an insight into what you might expect and come across whilst opening your mind to the possibility of making your money do some work for a change. It's simply what I've found to work the best. I'm not sponsored or endorsed by anyone, so you can be confident in the fact this is a completely independent resource. There is no hidden agenda.

I want to give you the tools to transform your life. This book will show you how to set up your first investment portfolio. None of this information means quitting the day job. You don't need money up front and you can fit all of this alongside your normal life. It'll also be a journey that your entire family can get involved in. Investing is a skill to pass down to the next generation to make sure your kids have the best chance to succeed in life. I'll transform the way you think about money so you can use it to its full potential to build your wealth; however, this is not a book that will show some magic get-rich-quick system or a fool-proof "winning" method. It requires commitment, discipline and a hunger to learn.

In the past when learning about investing, I became fed up with always having to do further homework despite reading a book that was supposed to be teaching me about that very topic! There were too many books that skipped over the basics, important terms and phrases were poorly explained or missed out entirely, so this book will change all of that. I'll lay out all the facts you need to know to start investing. I'll explain investment jargon using examples where possible. Ultimately, I'll walk you through how to set up your first investment. This is a true end-to-end learning resource. It'll enable you to make clear, informed decisions about investing, even if you know nothing at all about investing. There might be topics in this book that you already know, but I'd rather risk coming across patronising than you go through the frustration of not understanding something.

Investing is often seen as inaccessible for most people but that couldn't be further from the truth. You might be reading this thinking *"It's just gambling"* or *"I'd never risk my money like that"* and these wrong assumptions can put people off. Often, it's just the fear of the unknown. I had those same feelings when I started, but the more I learned, the more I understood, and the more I realised how much better investing was than just saving.

We're all born completely average. But as humans we're incredibly good at adapting. One of the very best things we do is learn and hopefully you'll learn a lot about investing. There are many books that have the impressive claim of *"This is the only book you'll need to read"* and I wouldn't dare make as bold a claim as that, but I can definitely say this is the book you need to read *first*.

What this book is not

It's important to draw the line between good and bad – and there's a lot of bad in the investment world, especially for beginners. This book isn't a list of "hot tips" on shares or companies. Investment tips are no different to tips on a racehorse – it's just gambling. Neither is this book a magic investing system that will miraculously earn you 1,000% returns in 10 days. I'm trying to introduce you to the concept of putting your money to work for you, not showing you how to gamble away your life savings. This book also isn't for anyone that's a short-term investor – commonly referred to as a "trader". I firmly believe the best way for anyone to become wealthy is to focus on long-term investing only and you'll see why as you read on. If you're looking for a quick-fix solution to your money woes, I'm sorry, but you're reading the wrong book.

This book isn't a recommendation to sell or buy any particular investment. Everything is based on my own personal circumstances and should be used to guide your decisions. I can guarantee it's filled with as much good information as I can fit in it to give someone a head-start. The whole point of this book is *you* learning how to do it, feeling confident enough to start and empowered. Nobody else knows your money better than you.

2 ABOUT ME

Most of these sections in books are filled with a big list of accomplishments of the person behind the words, or a fancy foreword from some world-renowned expert from the same topic of discussion. I don't have those things. First and foremost, I'm not a financial professional, but before you angrily get rid of this book, I'll explain why I'm perfectly placed to be writing about this material.

First of all, a bit about me. I'm a father of two and have a wonderful fiancée, Beth. We're a "normal" family – most of the time – and in my day job, I'm an engineering team leader working for an aerospace company. Outside of work, for nearly the last 7 years, my hardcore passion has been investing. It excites me that you can put your money to work just in the same way as you'd work yourself to build a better life for you and your family. I'm always doing research on the trends, technologies and companies of the future. It's a great feeling to be able to be a part of that by owning parts of those companies and profiting from their success. My investing journey started slowly and I had some early failures which I'll discuss in later chapters, but regardless of that I was hooked. The more things I tried, the more interested I became. The more topics I researched, the more I asked myself *"Just how far can I take this"*?

I began to realise the best ways – and the worst ways – to invest for someone getting started with a family. I recognise that you don't do this as part of a day job and might not even want to. Like how I invest, you can do this completely in your spare time and it'll fit around whatever you do for a living. Everything in this book takes those things into account. I had no money whatsoever and no knowledge of investing and if you're in the same situation that's totally fine. I'm trying to spread the message that investing isn't just confined to the rich or the elite. It really is accessible for normal families.

My engineering background compliments my investing hobby very well. It's allowed me to break down complex topics into easy-to-manage pieces and logically formulate steps to solve a problem. I've spent years analysing what works well and what doesn't. The types of investments, the method of investing, the frequency, the right investment providers, how much risk to take, how much it costs, you name it I've read about it and tried it. All the trial-and-error and the early mistakes mean I know exactly what you should be focusing on to transform your lives. I've written exactly the type of book that I wish existed when I started out.

You might think the time isn't right, or the odds are stacked against you, I know there are a lot of people going through a tough time in life, but the situation doesn't need to be perfect to take the first steps. When I first started, my partner was expecting our first child, my sassy, beautiful daughter. We were desperately trying to save every penny we could get our hands on for a house deposit. We were paying extortionate rent on a tiny one bedroom flat barely big enough for the both of us. I was nervous, unsure, but I realised something needed to change. Bringing my daughter into the world flicked a switch on in my head that made me realise I needed to renovate our lives.

It took me a lot of time. I absorbed as much information as I possibly could and still am to this day. There were dead-ends and false-starts before I started properly – and all I started with was just a few pounds a month. The price of one Starbucks coffee a week. Nowadays you can start with even less than that. Regardless of how much money you have spare right now, that early fostering of a small amount of discipline made it much easier for me to slowly crank up the contributions over time just like you'll be able to do. I'm looking forward to where my family's going to be in the next 10, 20, 30 years. I hope you can use the knowledge in my book to secure your family's financial future too.

3 WHAT IS INVESTING?

Starting from the basics, the term "investing" refers to the act of giving money to an organisation with the expectation of receiving income or profit in the future. You do this already with your time. When you go to work, whether you're self-employed or work for someone else, you invest your time and in return, someone deposits an amount of money in your bank account every few weeks. So, your time has monetary value. If you work a bit of overtime, or have another part-time job, you might take home a bit more money, but once that work is finished and you've worked your set hours, you can't earn any more money from trading your time. Investing makes your money work for *you* rather than just you work for money.

Instead of trading your time for money, wouldn't it be great if you could use it for something else like spending it with your family or hobbies you enjoy? The ultimate goal of investing is that your money ends up working just as hard, if not harder than you do. Your hours at work are no doubt long and require sacrifices at times. Investing is a way to make your money do some of this heavy lifting instead. It's also a way to set aside money while you're busy with other things and forget about it. What's even better, is that as it generates more money and that money is also put to work, over the years you can create extraordinary sums of money.

Why you can do a better job than a professional

The first thing many people think of when investing is *"Oh I better speak to a financial advisor"* but financial advisors are absolutely not essential for the average investor. This book is here to help you feel confident enough to learn about how investing works so you don't have to pay bucket loads of money to an advisor to tell you what to do with your own money. You might be tempted to use your bank's financial advice service because you feel they're more trustworthy than one selected at random or because it simplifies the process of looking for a good one, but there is no better financial advisor other than yourself. Nobody is going to be as focused and motivated to make the best of your money than you are.

Another issue with financial advice is banks often have a minimum earning or savings amount to even be considered for it. Lloyds and Halifax won't see you unless you earn at least £100,000 a year. The worst thing of all is that if you go to your bank for advice, you'll only ever get recommendations for *their* products. When you consider how many options you have in the investment world, that's laughably small. You're paying for advice but getting such a small amount of value from it because if a competitor has a better investment product, do you think they're going to recommend that? Of course not!

You really don't need to be giving your hard-earned cash to a financial adviser. You're just funnelling money into their wallet, because they get paid regardless of how your investments perform. What if they give you bad advice? Oh well, they're not losing any sleep or money over that.

If you're still not confident then by all means get financial advice. Independent financial advisers' fees vary depending on what they are charging you for and how you pay. The average UK financial advisor charges about £150 per hour. There are other charging structures in place such as set fees for a piece of work, monthly fees and percentage fees, but for the average investor this is poor value for money. Unless you have a really complex financial setup, already have lots of money to invest (well done!), or feel really uncomfortable about the prospect of picking your own investments, there's absolutely no good reason to be paying for one. The good resources are out there, you just have to find them. You've started in a good place with this book.

Introduction to the stock market

The basic principle of investing follows one of two streams. Either buy an asset and wait for it to gain in value, then sell it on for a profit, or receive an income in exchange for spending your money. Most forms of investing need a place where buyers and sellers meet to exchange money in return for investments. The stock market is a term used to describe this place. The stock market isn't a physical place, it's a loose network of transactions spread all over the world. Not every company is listed on the stock market as you need to meet certain criteria. In the UK, a company that is "publicly listed" means their shares are available to buy or sell on the stock market. You've probably seen the term "Plc" – publicly listed company –at the end of some company names.

You might come across the terms *"stock market"*, *"stock exchange"* and *"stock market index"* when investing. Each of these terms refers to different things in the investing world which you need to be aware of. There are lots of places that confuse the terms or use them interchangeably when they're subtly different.

The stock market is the main realm of investing. Just like a food market, it's the place where sellers sell and buyers buy. It contains all of the trading activity of all the buyers and sellers of most of the world's investments. It's not a physical place, it's more of a global network of all investment transactions.

A stock exchange is a smaller entity within the stock market which contains a smaller set of companies than the overall market. There are many different exchanges that exist in different parts of the world. For example, the New York Stock Exchange (NYSE) and the London Stock Exchange (LSE) has a selection of companies listed in their exchanges. When listed on a stock exchange, buyers and sellers can access these companies and invest in them.

A stock market index is another level down from a stock exchange and is effectively a glorified list of companies. The reason for the existence of stock indexes is that it's too difficult to track the performance of every single company from an entire industry so a stock market index takes a sample of companies grouped together by a particular theme and track the performance of them instead, which is more manageable to deal with.

You've probably heard of the main UK stock market indexes like the Financial Times Stock Exchange (FTSE) 100 and FTSE 250 – pronounced "footsie". These two indexes consist of the largest UK companies by market value. The FTSE 100 has the largest 100 companies, and the FTSE 250 has the largest 250, and by monitoring their performance you can see how UK companies as a whole are doing. Other index examples include the S&P 500 in the USA which is the 500 largest US companies and the Hang Seng Index lists the largest companies in Hong Kong. There are stock market indexes for regular companies but also more unusual stuff. There's an index called the Liv-ex Fine Wine 50 which tracks the daily price movement of the fine wine market, and there's even the STOXX Europe Football Index that covers all football clubs that are listed on a stock exchange in Europe. Stock market indexes are the basis for some of the most useful investing techniques for the beginner as you'll find out later on in the book.

Any number of things can influence the price of investments on the stock market. News articles, political issues, industrial action, technological breakthroughs, medical trial results, the list is endless. Almost anything and everything happening right now will influence the prices of some investment somewhere in the world.

Introduction to asset classes

We now know the stock market is the place where buyers and sellers meet, and what they sell are assets. Assets are sometimes called securities or equities and there are four main types of assets, called asset classes when investing. These are:

- Cash
- Shares (also known as stocks or equities)
- Bonds (also known as fixed-income investments)
- Property

An asset class is a group of similar investments that has similar characteristics and behaves in a similar way. For example, shares behave in a similar way whether you buy them from a British pharmaceutical company or an American oil mining company. We'll discuss the importance of not just focusing on one asset class later in the book, but for now – other than cash as we know what that is – here's a breakdown of each of the main asset classes.

Shares

Shares are one of the main asset classes when investing. They are often called shares or equities and are issued by companies that want to raise money to grow their business by other means than just through their business operations. The company will assess its value, divide that number into equal portions called "shares" and then offer some or all of them for sale on the open stock market. These can then be bought by us, who become shareholders.

The popular misconception related to shares is that many people think if you own shares of a company, you are a part-owner of that company. That not entirely true. You don't part-own a company you have bought shares in and you've no claim to any of the company's property or money. What shareholders own are the shares issued by the company. For example, if you owned shares in Vodafone, you couldn't walk into Vodafone's head office and demand any office furniture thinking that you owned a chair or desks-worth of shares. This is an important feature of shares because it ensures that Vodafone's property is legally separated from your own. If Vodafone was to go bankrupt, a court can force all of Vodafone's business assets to be sold to cover any debts it owes, but as a shareholder your personal assets aren't at risk.

So, what good are shares then if you don't actually own the company? When you buy a company's shares, you become a shareholder. Being a shareholder means you have a physical share in the company's *success*. You're entitled to a portion of the company's profits – called dividends and discussed later – and if the shares rise in value, you can sell them on for a profit. You're also entitled to vote in shareholder meetings. If you owned a lot of Vodafone's shares, your voting power increases so that you can control the company's direction by appointing the board of directors.

Bonds

Bonds are investments that represent the debt of a company. You might also come across the term "gilt". Gilts are just the name for bonds that are issued by the UK Government. Effectively they are loans or an I.O.U to the company that wants to use your money to help fund parts of their business. They are issued when companies or the government need to raise money.

When you buy a bond, you are effectively loaning out your money and become a "bondholder". In return for handing over your money, the government/company is required to pay you interest as well as your original loan amount back. The interest rate is called the bond "coupon rate" and the date at which your original loan amount is due to be paid back is called the "maturity" date.

Most normal bonds are fixed-income investments which mean the coupon rate stays the same until the maturity date, regardless of what's happening to interest rates in general in the economy. There can be good and bad points to this as you'll see when you read on, but they are less risky than shares as a bondholder is always ahead of the queue in front of shareholders if a business goes bankrupt and you want a claim to your money. Bonds are also still tradeable assets like shares are, so whilst the rate of return is fixed with a bond, you're not stuck with a bond after you've bought it. You can sell it on to others.

Property

The obvious way to invest in property is to buy a house and rent it out, but that's mostly out of reach for everyday investors. It also comes with its own issues such as problem tenants and repair costs. Property prices and demand for rentals can go up and down, so property is almost always a long-term investment. As you'll see later in the book, it's still possible to invest in property without having to buy any buildings.

4 THREE REASONS TO INVEST INSTEAD OF SAVE

So now you know a bit about what sorts of investments you'll be buying, let's go over in detail why you should be investing instead of saving. What's wrong with good old-fashioned savings accounts? After all everyone does it right? You know by now my thoughts are that to provide the best kind of financial future for your family, there's nothing more powerful than investing your money, but you still might not be convinced of that yet. This section will really get to the reason why you should be investing in the first place. I'm going to explore the reasons and give examples of why your savings will be worth less over time, how the hidden cost of inflation is much higher than the official figures would have you believe and why your pension (if you have one) should never be the only money relied upon for the Golden Years of your life.

It's no secret that the interest rates for savers in the UK has been terrible for years. Despite two interest rate rises to the Bank of England's base rate – the rate which all other savings rates are based on – interest rates for savers have actually decreased over the past eight years. The base rate rose to 0.5% in November 2017, then again to 0.75% in August 2018 but average interest rates were just 0.88% in November 2018. Most banks aren't passing that money to their loyal savers, so there's never been a better time to put your money to work elsewhere.

Longer term than that, the situation is even worse. If you look back over the past 50 years, annual interest rates on cash in the UK have been an average of 1.4% a year, but if you'd invested in shares, you'd have earned an average of 5.6% a year. Cash is good for short-term investing where you'll be paying for stuff very soon, but the sooner you start investing, the sooner you have an opportunity to earn some life changing sums of money.

Reason # 1 – The abomination of inflation

Even while it's sitting apparently safe-and-sound in a bank, there can be a hidden thief nabbing your hard-earned cash. Chances are you haven't even noticed. The enemy here is inflation. Inflation is the drip slowly leaking from the sink. You probably won't notice the effects immediately, but once you realise how much of an effect it can have on your finances, don't ignore it because over time it can do devastating things.

Within the context of money, the Cambridge dictionary defines inflation as *"an increase in prices over time, causing a reduction in the value of money"*. This means that as the years go by, the value or "purchasing power" of your money is slowly reducing because goods and services continuously get more expensive each year. Let's explore how this happens and crucially why real inflation is much higher than the fantasy figure quoted in official statistics.

Increase costs of living

You may have heard some headline-making statistics regarding RPI (retail price index) and CPI (consumer price index). There is also CPIH (Consumer price index including housing costs). All of these are measures of inflation within the UK. It's how the government keeps track of how fast prices are rising. They all broadly follow the same concept, but CPIH takes into account cost of housing where the others don't, so this is the one we're interested in. CPIH is an official measurement in line with European regulations. It's measured by using an imaginary "basket" of shopping to benchmark the cost of typical goods and services most commonly bought by households in that year. As the price of the individual items in the basket changes annually, so does the total cost of that imaginary basket, which is how inflation is tracked over time.

Each item in the basket is what we call "weighted" by the spend of a typical household budget and their individual contributions lead to the average CPIH inflation figure. This was 2.3% as of May 2018. It ultimately means that the average price of the basket has increased by 2.3%, so something previously costing £100 would now on average cost £102.30 – 2.3% more than the previous year. Increasing prices are one of the reasons nobody is going to get wealthy just by saving cash in a low-interest bank account.

The chart below uses petrol prices as an example why this average inflation figure, which you'll find referenced in all major headlines and news stories, is meaningless to track the *real* cost to customers. Using a giant basket to track inflation means certain assumptions have to be made, one of them is how much the average family spends on petrol. This spend on fuel is factored into the calculations that make up the 2.3% CPIH figure. If for example, like much of the UK, you spend a significant portion of your budget on fuel getting to and from work, the actual amount of fuel you use won't be reflected right in the weighting of the CPIH figure, and this would end up costing you more money. The real cost of fuel price rises as per Figure 1 is 10% in 18 months.

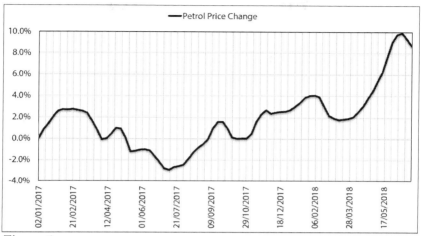

Figure 1

This isn't just the case for petrol, the same applies for other major necessary expenses such as food and energy. At the time of writing, the Big Six energy suppliers in Table 1 (British Gas, EDF, Scottish Power, Npower, SSE and E.ON) have recently announced price rises of their standard variable tariffs that are above the average level of inflation. If you have a young family like me and you use a high proportion of your income on your energy bills or you live in a cold part of the UK, this will also be under-represented in the overall inflation figure as you'll have a higher weighting of fuel use than the average.

Supplier	2018 Price Rise
British Gas	5.50%
EDF	2.70%
Scottish Power	5.50%
Npower	5.30%
SSE	6.70%
E.ON	2.60%

Table 1

Decreased savings

Inflation doesn't just make the price of things go up; it also makes the value of your savings go down. It's chipping away at all of your hard-earned money. Let's work through an example to understand a bit more. Imagine you had deposited £1000 in a UK bank account at the start of 2010. Let's assume this paid the average UK savings account interest rate each year until 2017. Here is the interest you would earn, shown in Table 2.

Initial deposit	£1,000	Ignoring the effect of inflation							
Year	2010	2011	2012	2013	2014	2015	2016	2017
Average UK Savings Account Interest Rates	2.80%	2.75%	2.80%	1.77%	1.48%	1.40%	1.23%	1.00%
Cumulative Interest per year	£1,028	£1,056	£1,085	£1,105	£1,121	£1,137	£1,151	£1,162

Table 2

You would have earned £162. Seems ok at first glance doesn't it? Not much earned, but better than nothing right? Let's now factor inflation into the picture to see the real effect on your money over that time. Table 3 shows the revised numbers with inflation included.

Initial deposit	£1,000	Including the effect of inflation							
Year	2010	2011	2012	2013	2014	2015	2016	2017
Average UK Savings Account Interest Rates	2.80%	2.75%	2.80%	1.77%	1.48%	1.40%	1.23%	1.00%
Average UK Inflation rate	3.30%	4.50%	2.80%	2.60%	1.50%	0.00%	0.70%	2.70%
Real rate of money growth	-0.50%	-1.75%	0.00%	-0.83%	-0.02%	1.40%	0.53%	-1.70%
Real value of cash per year after accounting for inflation	£995	£978	£978	£969	£969	£983	£988	£971

Table 3

When you include inflation, despite earning an extra £162.62, you see that the value of your initial £1000 after 7 years is only £971.26. This happens because we add the savings rate percentage to the inflation rate percentage. The growth in the value of your savings is cancelled out by the growth in inflation.

In 2010 for example, 2.8% interest + 3.3% inflation = - 0.5% interest. Your £1000 shrinks in value by 0.5% so it can only buy £995 worth of goods or services and by 2017, this has dropped even lower to £971! Due to inflation, everything else has risen in price by more money than you have earned in savings. Whilst the number in your bank account might still be going up, the *value* of that money has gone down, meaning you've effectively lost money.

Research from HM Revenue and Customs shows despite this poor return on cash, money is still pouring into cash Individual Savings Accounts (ISAs) all over the UK. And we're talking seriously big money. In the last year, 11 million adults put £39.1 billion in cash into UK ISAs. This represents over 75% of all ISA accounts, meaning only roughly 1 in 4 people who have ISAs are investing their money rather than saving it.

The example above shows a fairly short time-frame of 7 years, but the long-term effect of holding onto cash means you could be missing out on a lot of money. If your £1,000 was put into a cash ISA when they were launched in 1999, it would now be worth £1,204. If that same £1,000 had been invested in UK shares, on average it would now be worth 38% more at £1,663. Going back further than that, the situation is even worse still! The Barclays Equity Guilt Study from 2016 showed that since records began in 1899, saving cash has earned you a measly average of 0.8% per year. UK shares on the other hand have returned an average of 5.1%. These numbers include the effect of inflation, so it really does pay to invest.

Many people assume cash is safe in the bank. These numbers are why I disagree with that assumption. There is a real, hidden cost of doing nothing with your money. This is why investing is so important. You might think that investments are too risky, but there is also a real risk to keeping your cash in a low interest savings account when considering the financial future of you and your family.

In a way it's understandable that so many more people prefer saving over investing. The stock market craziness during the financial crisis of 2008 is still fresh in peoples' minds. But by keeping all of your cash in your bank account, you're at the mercy of poor interest rates and inflation. Other than for emergencies, I keep as little as possible in bank accounts and I'd encourage you to do similar. People often perceive any and all investments as high risk but there are many ways to manage your risk. See "Asset Allocation" and "Diversification" in Chapter 12.

Reason #2 – Pensions time-bomb

Another of the main reasons for investing for your family is the shocking condition of the UK pension landscape. The painful fact is that millions of people won't have enough money for retirement to enjoy even a mediocre standard of living. Imagine the pain of not being able to financially help your children as much as you want later on in life because you have barely enough money to live on in retirement. Or you face spending your twilight years in poverty because you never built up a big enough investment pot and pension through your life. Many people in the UK are looking at a retirement living, quite literally, in complete and utter poverty and yes – this could apply to you too. I want you to start *now* to build your wealth, so you're not facing a bleak retirement or missing out on finally being able to enjoy your hard-earned rest at the end of your working life.

At its core, this book is about improving your investing knowledge. It's not just for advice on pensions but nevertheless I still need to talk about them and how there are big problems with the way the pension system is set up today. Recent data shows that almost 1 in 3 UK adults has absolutely no private pension provision at all. Not a single bean.

Most of the information in this section is related to defined contribution and not defined benefit (sometimes called final salary) pensions. Most younger workers won't be on defined benefit pensions any more. My own pension is defined contribution and if yours is too, you're already an investor without even realising! A defined contribution pension will be invested in the stock market and effectively it works just like an investment portfolio, so using the knowledge you gain, it's your responsibility to make sure you're getting as much money out of it as possible.

The true cost of retirement

Many people probably aren't aware of the colossal sizes of pensions needed for a good standard of life in retirement. Let's go through some numbers. In 2017 the UK government published data that showed how much income in retirement you'd need just to maintain your current lifestyle. These pension pot sizes factor a reduced cost of certain types of things e.g. assuming the kids have left home (hopefully!) and any mortgages paid off but it also accounts for extra spend on more recreational activities or holidays. Looking at Table 4, if your earnings before retirement were £27,000 – roughly the UK average salary – then the government thinks you will need 67% of that salary in retirement just to keep your current lifestyle the same. That's the same amount of luxuries, going-out, essentially all the fun stuff. This means your target income each year in retirement is £18,090, about £1,500 a month. If you applied for and successfully received the full state pension – currently £164.35 a week – then you would need to find an extra £795 a month to get your target income of £18,090 a year. This is where your workplace or personal pension comes into play. An annuity, which is a fixed sum of money paid each year for the rest of your life, would cost you anywhere between £190,000 and £389,000.

This is also assuming you do get the full state pension at the time, otherwise you face having to pay even more to make up the difference. It's a big amount of money and that's all to just keep your standard of living *the same*. What about wanting a better life for you and your family? Enjoying all of those holidays and luxuries you've worked your whole life for? Unless you have that sort of money lying around already, you need to start putting it away now.

Earnings before retirement	Earnings Percentage needed to maintain lifestyle	Target retirement income per year	Monthly income needed on top of full state pension	Approximate annuity cost at age 65
£27,000	67%	£18,090	£795	£190,876
£56,000	50%	£28,000	£1,621	£389,076

Table 4

What's even more concerning is that despite the figures needed in Table 4, the average UK pension pot size is just £50,000. That'll buy you a pension worth about £2500 a year or just £208 a month. When you look at it visually in Figure 2 the differences are shocking. I'm not sure about you but I think I'd want to be spending a lot more than £208 a month when I retire. Either that or get used to beans and hotdogs for dinner. What a terrible way to spend your twilight years. It's a terrible situation but you're fortunate enough to be able to take steps to do something about it now.

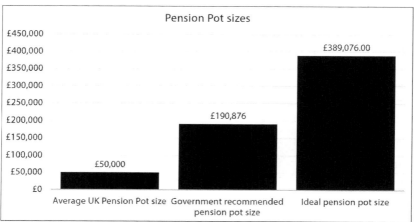

Figure 2

Depending on your age there's a very real chance of having to work until you're almost in your 70s. In 2017 the government raised the retirement age to 68 starting in the year 2037. This was 7 years earlier than it was supposed to be and reflects the large increase in number of people reaching pensionable age in the future. There could even be a situation in the future which means the State Pension doesn't exist. I'm fearful of that for my own kids so I'm taking steps now to make sure they're prepared. It's never been more important to take care of your family's finances rather than just rely on the state pension in the hope of keeping up the same standard of living. Make sure you're putting you and your family's best interests at heart by investing.

Whether you work for a company or are self-employed, there are certain things you should be doing right now with your existing pension. First and foremost, make sure you have one. Remember, almost 1 in 3 UK adults have no private pension at all. I can't stress this enough. It's so easy to ignore the situation now but as we've seen, you need every penny of your money working as hard as possible and a well-funded pension pot is absolutely essential.

<u>FREE money from the government and your employer</u>

Yes, completely free money and without a catch. In the past, many eligible workers missed out on valuable pension benefits because their employer didn't offer them one. Automatic enrolment changed all of that. As of 2017, every employer in the UK is legally required to put staff into a company pension scheme and contribute towards it as well as you. You may not realise you're in a pension scheme, but automatic enrolment is the absolute bare minimum of a workplace pension.

One of the most overlooked perks of workplace pensions is that you're getting free money in two different ways. The first lot of free money, assuming you're a basic rate tax payer (earning less than £46,350), comes from the 20% you save in tax on your pension contributions. Instead of that 20% going into the government's pot, that 20% tax is added into your pension pot. The government likes to give you a reward for saving for your future. It only costs you 80p for every £1 that goes into your pension. The second lot of free money is that as well as the government adding to your pension via tax relief, your employer adds to your pension too. Both of these contributions are at absolutely no extra cost to you. Table 5 below shows the legal minimums for you, the government and your employer contributing into your pension pots.

Date	Employee minimum Contribution	Government Contribution	Employer Minimum Contribution	Total Minimum Contribution
Currently, from 6 April 2018 to 5 April 2019	2.4% (from your own pocket)	+0.6% Free (the tax you're saving)	+2% Free (that your employer pays into your pot)	2.4% from you + 0.6% from the government + 2% employer = 5% total
6 April 2019 onwards	4% (from your own pocket)	+1% Free (the tax you're saving)	+3% Free (that your employer pays into your pot)	4% from you + 1% from the government + 3% employer = 8% total

Table 5

From 6th of April 2019, you'll have to contribute 4% minimum, but this is easily made back as your money will be doubled to 8%.

Don't opt-out!

You have the ability to opt-out of your employer's pension and you might have already done so. Maybe you're thinking "*I need the money too much now, 4% of my salary is a lot*" and I completely understand, but let's consider an example about how much free money you'd miss out on if you opted out of auto-enrolment. Here's our imaginary friend Dave:

- Dave is 20 years old in April 2019 and plans to retire at 65.
- Dave could afford to save the minimum auto-enrolment figures (4% personal, 1% tax saving, 3% employer) for his whole working life.
- Dave earns £27,000 a year (not bad for a 20-year-old), with a 1% yearly increase in pay every year.
- Dave decides to opt-out of his workplace pension.

I've assumed a couple of things in this example:

- Any interest is paid annually
- The growth of Dave's investment pot is a fairly pessimistic and very achievable 2% per year average.

Now let's fast-forward to Dave's retirement. As per Figure 3, if Dave had *not* decided to opt-out of his workplace pension, over the course of his working life, he could have made a fantastic pension pot size of £199,643 – easily meeting the government recommended pension pot size of £190,000 from Table 4. Half of his entire contributions, a massive £62,689 came from his employer and the government, but Dave chose to opt-out of auto-enrolment so missed out on all that lovely free money.

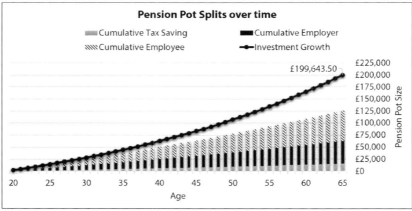

Figure 3

The average pension figure of £50,000 seems like a lot of money, but for a good quality retirement, it's terrible. A good pension is easily achievable provided you take steps sooner rather than later. There's no real reason to miss out on these contributions from employers, especially when they're legally required to pay them on your behalf, so make sure you don't opt out of your workplace pension. Don't be like Dave.

<u>Tweak your workplace pension if needed</u>

Many work place pension providers now have easily manageable online portals for checking on the performance of your defined contribution pension. It's effectively like online banking but for pensions. You often don't have to wait until you get your annual pension statement through in the post.

If you have a workplace pension, ask your employer if they give you online access. If they do, check it and ask yourself, is it enough? Many employers also give the option to edit which types of investments make up part of your pension. Remember, a defined contribution pension is effectively an investment portfolio that you can't touch until you retire. The investments that your pension is invested in will most likely have been chosen by your employer but it doesn't mean they're the best suited to your personal circumstances, and you may want to change them if you can.

My employer gives me the option to pick between 6 different investment funds of increasing levels of risk, enabling me to tailor my investments throughout my life based on my current tolerance to risk so check if yours does the same. There's more about risk in the next chapter. Make sure, above all your workplace pension is right for you, and if it's not, take steps to do something about it.

<u>If you're self-employed</u>

Things are a little different if you're self-employed, but the basic principles are the same. You don't have the fortune of an employer to add to your pension pot but you're still entitled to free money from the government via savings on tax. You'll need a Personal Pension. We go through these in Chapter 8, so don't worry, I've got you covered.

Reason #3 – Supercharging your quality of life

This is probably the most important reason of all. You might be thinking *"You've talked a lot about pensions, shouldn't I just be paying more into that?"*. If so, good point. While pensions are important, retirement should never be your main goal. Life paths are not set in stone. Why build all your wealth over decades only to have to finish your working life to enjoy it? I didn't just write this book for you to give yourself a better pension. I want you to achieve a better quality of life *as soon as possible*, by using investments as the vehicle to do it.

Most people already have a good idea about what they'd do with more money. Wouldn't it be fantastic if you could put the deposit down for that new house, buy that new car, go on that luxury holiday? If like me you have young kids, you're probably wondering how to provide the best possible life for them as you watch them grow up. What if you didn't have to think of future university fees or to make sure they don't have to go through the same hardships you went through?

Any and all of those things are absolutely possible providing you put in the work now and start building up your investment portfolio. You have two choices, you can work harder, or you can make your *money* work harder. This book is your starting point. Everything I talk about in this book is achievable and specifically designed for regular working people like you and me. Use it as the first stepping stone. Read it, absorb it and start investing. I think you'll surprise yourself.

5 IGNORE THIS CHAPTER AT YOUR OWN RISK

Risk is one of the most misunderstood and exaggerated parts of investing. This chapter will bust some of the myths with investing and explore a bit more about what risk actually is. I'll also help you discover how adventurous of an investor you are and why being too cautious can be just as bad as being too risky. When you understand how risks can impact your finances, you can lower your fears against them and make clearer decisions to help you invest in the right things.

What is risk?

There are several definitions of risk depending on where you look. The Oxford dictionary has a general definition which says risk is a *"situation involving exposure to danger"* or from a financial perspective, *"the possibility of financial loss"* with the danger obviously being your lost money. I prefer defining risk in the same way it's defined on Wikipedia, which is *"the likelihood of gaining or losing something of value"* as this recognises – very importantly – that there is actually a positive side to risk as well as a negative side. It's the negative side that gets the most attention as it can cause the most damage, but a key point to remember is that in most situations there's a chance of a good outcome and a bad outcome.

If you were to ask someone if they'd consider investing their money, more often than not, their immediate response would be *"Oh, I wouldn't dream of doing that, it's far too risky"*. When most people think about investing and risk, they give unnatural emphasis to all of the apparently terrible things that are going to happen to their money. Nobel prize winner and behavioural psychologist Daniel Kahneman, discussed this in his book "Thinking fast and slow" that humans give much more emphasis on the bad that can happen rather than the good.

He showed this is a fundamental part of human-nature:

"Humans in general are hardwired to minimize threats rather than maximise opportunities."

Stemming from our hunter-gatherer days, this made sense. Minimising immediate threats to survival was always more important than maximising the amount of long-term resources available. Humans were much more "short-termist" because we had to be to stay alive. We are hard-wired to be "risk-averse" and shy away from perceived threats. This still exists today at a biological level and so we give much greater emphasis on minimising bad stuff than maximising god stuff whether we want to or not. It's literally in our DNA. It's even entrenched into the English language for how we use the word "risk" in sentences. We might talk about the *"risks of dying in a plane crash"* but you never hear people talk about *"the risk of winning the lottery"*, despite there being a very real – small – chance of either of those things happening. One is obviously much more positive than the other!

In modern day England in the context of your finances, we aren't exposed to the same life-threatening situations our ancestors once were. The hard-wired nature of how we deal with risk ends up influencing how we deal with money. There's never a good reason to put yourself in a position to lose all of your money, but by trying to avoid financial threats too much, such as companies going bankrupt or markets crashing, too many people end up being too cautious. When it comes to savings versus investments, almost 50% of people in the UK want to avoid investment risks at all costs. There's a term to describe that and it's called "reckless caution" which means acting so cautious in your daily life that it's detrimental to achieving your goals. We actively minimise the likelihood of good returns on our money because we're scared of losing it all.

Risks exist in everyday life and in everything we do, even in the seemingly mundane things. Flush the word "guaranteed" from your mind right now. Do you think driving to work is risk-free? The odds of getting into an accident are 1 in 17,500. Right now, there are currently over 1 million near-earth asteroids in orbit larger than 37 metres that would cause major damage if they hit earth. The odds of dying when falling out of bed? 1 in about 2 million! The point I'm trying to make is that even us *existing* on earth isn't risk free. That doesn't mean life is a bad thing though, does it? It's all in the perceptions. Clint Eastwood once said:

"If you want a guarantee, go and buy a toaster."

Many people perceive banks as a safe place for their money, but they're a business like any other. They can and do go bust, so they're not risk-free either. Although the UK Financial Services Compensation Scheme (FSCS) covers your savings up to £85,000 for deposits. Investments are also covered but only if you receive financial advice which includes bad advice, poor investment management or misrepresentation and negligence claims relating to mis-selling of pensions.

Risks are unavoidable, but as far as investing is concerned, there are ways to manage it so you're doing it at the level you're comfortable with. You may already have an assumption on how risky or risk-averse you are based on your current goals in life. We'll find out more about that now.

Identifying your Risk Appetite

Your risk appetite is where your own personal tolerance for risk sits on the risk spectrum. This is an entirely personal decision about how adventurous or cautious you are when picking your investments. Some types of investments are considered safer than others – some I wouldn't necessarily call "investments" at all, more like gambling. As a DIY investor like yourself, you need to start to think about what kind of appetite you have so you can invest in things that are right for you.

Your risk appetite will depend mostly on your life goals, how soon you want to achieve them and your age. Someone who is 22, has a major part of their working life ahead of them and happens to want to buy a Ferrari, will need to invest very differently than someone who is 57, just about to retire and has children that'll be wanting some cash for a house deposit soon.

Riskier investments mean there's a higher risk of losing money, so the chances are slim that you want 100% of your portfolio in high-risk investments when you're just about to retire. You might end up with a wild swing in the value of your investments which could hamper your retirement plans. I'm not for one second suggesting that younger investors must be riskier and older investors must be safer, but the wants and needs of these two types of investors is going to be different. Be critical of yourself though. Focus while thinking about this and really push yourself to try and maximise the level of risk you're willing to take, even if that means doing it with a smaller chunk of your investment pot. It's really easy to go *"I'll just stick to low-risk stuff"* but you might be missing out on major monetary gains over the years and you might even unintentionally be risking more than you thought. This is an important trap with your risk appetite that you need to avoid.

Let's imagine you think of yourself as one of the 50% of people who doesn't want to invest at all and keep financial risks at a minimum. You're 25 years old and your main goal in life is to save up as much money as possible in low-interest bank accounts with the aim of retiring early at 45. Now this clearly isn't achievable for most normal people by savings alone. If you try and protect your finances too much by being recklessly cautious, your overall focus on lowering your financial risks by not investing your money is actually a *high-risk* strategy, not a low-risk one. This is because you've just lowered your chances of getting enough money to actually achieve your life goal of retiring early. It seems counter-intuitive but it's true. The measure of risk often isn't a financial one, it's the risk of you not achieving one of your life's main goals, which is something much bigger than money.

Your risk appetite depends on how "emotionally tolerant" you are. For example, if prices of shares in your investment portfolio were to drop sharply overnight, would you be cool about it knowing you were confident in your original decisions? Or would you panic and act irrationally? If you're emotionally tolerant, you're able withstand the emotional effects of price fluctuations and you might want riskier investments to take advantage of this tolerance. If you can't bear to think about your investments swinging in value wildly over the years, then maybe you want to stick to the lower-risk stuff so you don't run the risk of losing all your hair and sanity.

There's no right or wrong choice with this, but you need to think about your appetite now and review it regularly – at least once you've finished this book, but at the very minimum once a year. Attitudes and life-goals change over time and yours could too.

To help determine your risk appetite, first ask yourself the following questions:

- When you read the title of this chapter and the word "risk", did you associate the word with danger, uncertainty, opportunity or thrill?
- Would you prefer more job security and a small pay increase or less job security and a big pay increase?
- How easily do you adapt when things go wrong?
- Would a friend or family member consider you as risky?
- Are there risky things you've thought about doing in the past and if so, did you do them, or what stopped you doing them?

Now compare your attitude to finance against the categories in Table 6 below. These are the broad categories of investors that I've made for this book. The aim is for you to identify which of those categories best fits with your appetite for risk so that when you read the rest of the book, you're familiar with the types of assets you should be focusing on. Most investors will fit within one of these categories but there may be some that flex and move. This isn't an exam. There's no right or wrong answer.

	The different types of investor
D	**Defensive Only Investors** They target keeping the current value of their money over anything else. Their investments will have a big amount as cash deposits, but with a small amount invested in low-risk investments to try and keep at or slightly above the level of inflation. This will be the least volatile type but also the likely lowest return (if any). My hope is that even if this is you now, after reading this book it opens your eyes to aiming for more than this.
C	**Cautious Investors** They target small levels of growth with a portfolio of investments that are lower risk. They will mainly focus on fixed-interest investments and defensive shares in the UK market. This may also include property via REITs (See Chapter 8). They are fine with a bit of volatility in the short-term but not long-term (greater than 5 years).
B	**Balanced Investors** They target longer-term investment growth and are happy with higher (but not too high) levels of risk. Investments will be mainly in fixed-interest ones such as bonds, with a focus on the UK market. They are happier with a small amount of "alternative", riskier investment types of investments to compliment the "safer" ones (See Chapter 8). They are fine with a moderate amount of volatility in the short-term (less than 5 years).
G	**Growth Investors** They target long-term investment growth by investing with medium-to-high levels of risk. They're more comfortable with investments from overseas and "alternative" investments that have a greater opportunity for growing their money. They're more comfortable with volatility in the short and medium term.
A	**Adventurous Investors** They target high, long-term investment growth by investing in assets with high levels of risk. Their investments will mostly be overseas and "alternative". They expect and are comfortable with a lot of volatility to achieve high levels of return over the long term.
S	**Speculative Investors** They target the highest level of investments with little care for issues that may affect their assets. Their investments will be global and many, if not all, of their portfolio will be alternative investments with a very high level of volatility to try and achieve the highest return over the long term.

Table 6

Depending on your attitude and goals, there will be certain investment products better suited than others. My custom risk ratings are a categorising tool to help you consider what types of investments to consider. Look for these icons in other places of the book as I'll be using them to help you decide on the types of investments that might be suitable for you.

The risk of not doing anything

The final point on risk I want to make is the risk of inaction. Let's suppose you go to the beach with your family. It's a lovely day and you go and set up right near the shoreline. The weather's good, sun's out and everyone's having fun. Kids are playing with a bat and ball, making sandcastles and swimming in and out of the sea. You're completely absorbed by your music/book/magazine, you know the kids are safe as you can hear them in the background. Suddenly you notice your towel getting wet. You look up and the tide has come in. You're about to get cut off by the water and need to scramble quickly back to your car, wet clothes and kids in hand. You didn't do anything differently, you didn't move or anything, but the situation had changed *around* you and by doing nothing in that changing situation you've unexpectedly exposed yourself to some inconveniences and danger. Risk is not just based on the "doing" of things. The risk in that situation was to simply to do nothing at all. This is the risk of inaction.

By not actively putting your money to work for you, you're risking missing out on any fantastic gains as your investments grow over the years. You'll never see it happening though. It shows itself as years of wasted opportunities and a smaller cash pot in retirement. There's a name for this and it's similar to reckless caution. It's called "shortfall risk". This means failing to meet your financial goals because the return you have made on your money is too low. This could be a complete disaster in retirement. Can you imagine running out of money and having to look for other ways to finance your lifestyle when all you want to do is enjoy and relax? The thought terrifies me, and I hope this chapter has you thinking about what sort of risks you're comfortable with.

6 SAVE OVER £7,500 A YEAR TO INVEST

Wanting to invest is fantastic but anyone needs cash to be able to buy those investments. Rather than assume you have money lying around already – and I never did when I started – I've made a list of some obvious and not-so-obvious ways you can start freeing up cash. I've also used all of these methods personally and they've worked very well. My main goal in writing this section was minimising the impact of these changes as much as possible. I don't want you to be living off tins of beans and baked potatoes. These steps are easy, practical and fit into everyday life. That's the most important point of all – they have to work for you or they're not much use.

Set a family budget

The Office for National Statistics report for the end of 2017 shows that as a nation we're spending more than ever. The average amount spent by each family in the UK was £553.20 per week which was the most expensive year since 2006. It's a crazy amount of money. One of the first steps to taking control of your finances and before you invest any money at all should be a family budget. It will take a little bit of effort to set one up if you've not done one before, but this will make all the difference.

The thing that really opened my eyes to the importance of family budgeting was about a year or so into my investment journey. There never seemed to be enough cash at the end of the month and we thought we had a pretty good idea of spending, but at the time had no formal budget in place. It originally had me worried and I thought *"Surely we aren't spending that much money? What's there to show for it?"*. As a family, we went over our monthly spend with a fine-tooth comb and realised that over just one month, there was hundreds of pounds worth of totally unnecessary spend. It was all small, one-off purchases; sandwiches, coffees, trinkets, all of it was under £15 and none of it was essential whatsoever.

Addressing this issue by setting up an actual budget drastically changed the situation overnight. We'd freed up hundreds of pounds a month, just by spending less on stuff that didn't even matter in the first place. That was just the thing about those types of purchases, none of them whatsoever were meaningful. If you'd asked me to pick 5 things from a list, I wouldn't have even remembered what they were. There's big power in setting a budget as a family. It'll show you exactly what you should be spending on things and on what types of things you need to lower your spending on.

The Money Advice Service has an excellent free, easy-to-use budget planner which is available on their website. Money Saving Expert also has a fantastic and in-depth guide called The Money Makeover. There's also more information on all the digital investment helpers in Chapter 8 which can automate some of this process, but for now, to get you started, here are the basic steps to setting up a good budget.

What is your monthly income?

This should be fairly basic but not everyone knows exactly how much they have coming in per month, especially if you're working irregular hours or your earnings are based on commission. Use best estimates where you can for each month in the year. Divide the total by 12 to give you a monthly average. It doesn't need to be down to the penny, but you need to establish a baseline income so you can compare it against your expenses.

What are your fixed expenses per month?

These are things that don't usually vary from month-to-month. Things such as rent, mortgage, loans, insurance, fuel or utility bills provided you pay by direct debit are all classed as fixed expenses. Whilst they don't vary now from month-to-month, you might be able to identify some areas for improvement in your fixed expenses, especially with items like utility bills and insurance when it's up for renewal.

What are your variable expenses per month?

These are things that usually do vary from month-to-month. Food shopping, restaurant visits, entertainment, clothes and gifts will all vary throughout the year, especially with birthdays. Include utility bills in here if you currently don't pay by direct debit, as you'll likely pay more for your utilities in winter than you do in the summer months if you're on a normal tariff. Try and plan ahead for the year, anticipating spend around the holidays and for special occasions. When you have a yearly total, average it by dividing by 12 to give you your variable expenses per month.

Compare your expenses and income

This is a simple comparison between your fixed and variable expenses against your income and is calculated as follows.

Monthly income – (fixed expenses per month + variable expenses per month) = monthly surplus or deficit.

Are you in the positive or the negative? You should hopefully be in a position where you're not spending more than you earn, but if you're not, you're likely paying for regular living costs with a form of credit, which is never going to be good for your long-term wealth. You might instinctively know this already, but it's important to know just how much money you have left over, especially if you're regularly paying off credit card payments as part of your overall expenses.

Evaluate and adjust

Once you've baselined your current situation, you can start thinking about any adjustments to make, especially if it's given you a surprise where you thought you were spending less than you actually were. You might find that you can cut back in a few areas, but you realise you need more money in others. The first time we did our budget properly, I was amazed how much petrol I used for work. There wasn't much I could do about it given the location of my job and the nature of the travel, but it meant we could budget the money for it accordingly and not have a shock at the end of the month.

How to free up cash

Now that you've defined your initial budget, use this list as a prompt to start to free up money to invest. Pick at the very least five of these suggestions and give them a go for two months. When you can physically see the cold, hard cash in your bank account this is a very powerful motivator and I'm hopeful you'll continue. It's an even better feeling when you consider the very reason that you're saving this money is to put it to work with the aim of making even more money. Even if you don't or can't make all of the changes listed below, I hope its eye opening and inspires you to think of things that I might have missed off this list.

Make your coffee at home

Like most adults, especially with kids, I can't function without a morning fix of caffeine. It can be quite traumatic commuting to and from work without it. If you're a daily coffee drinker who prefers buying rather than making your coffee, you're spending a lot over the year for something easy, quick and very, very cheap to make yourself at home. Not only are you helping the environment by not buying those awful single-use coffee cups, you'll save a small a fortune. The average price of a UK takeaway coffee from the likes of Starbucks, Nero or Costa will cost about £2.50 a day. Assuming you have one every weekday day of the year, that's a cost of £650. Instant coffee on the other hand, only costs a staggering 6p per cup on average, meaning you're saving £634 a year just on coffee.

Yearly Saving: £634

Skip the drinks at restaurants

Saving money has to be realistic. It'll obviously save a tonne of money if you stop going to restaurants completely but it'll also suck any of the fun out of investing if you're giving up too much to fund it. A surprisingly easy way we save money while still enjoying a meal out is to skip the alcoholic drinks. Alcoholic drinks are crazily overpriced at restaurants and add major cost to your bill. If Beth and I are having 2 drinks each during the course of the meal, where beers are £4+ and glasses of wine are £5+ in most UK restaurants, that's an extra £18 and pretty much like paying for a 3rd guest's main course. Nobody likes a tag-along on a date, especially a financial one. A great alternative to expensive drinks at restaurants is just a simple lemon-wedge in some table water, which in most places, costs nothing at all. If you go out for food once a month, this simple switch would save over £200 a year. Or if you must have alcohol, try a cheaper alternative – perhaps a gin and soda water/lemonade rather than a more expensive cocktail and limit it to one only.

Yearly Saving: £216

Haggle/Compare on your contracts

Haggling or using comparison sites can save you lots of money. Research from consumer association Which? showed that with the list of services and products in Table 7, for just a few phone calls to challenge the price, or to hop onto a website, you could be onto a winner. With regards to haggling, the key to a successful haggle is showing that you can get what you want cheaper somewhere else, and that you're happy to follow through and go to the alternative source. After all, most sellers would rather keep you as a customer than lose the sale altogether. More guidance can be found on the Which? website at www.which.co.uk.

Product	Savings up to
Car Breakdown cover	£35
Home Insurance	£40
Car Insurance	£50
Phone contracts	£72
Broadband and subscription TV	£216
Energy Bills	£312

Table 7

Yearly Saving: £725

Shift your debt to a 0% card

Credit cards are a natural part of life for many people, but you should only ever use 0% interest credit cards. With a young family of my own, I know better than anyone that it's easier to put things on a credit card with a 0% introductory rate when the kids are young, especially with all the stress going on, the toys and clothes to buy. But don't forget about that card, because when the 0% deal is over, the interest rate will skyrocket. It's so easy to switch to a 0% deal these days, there's no excuse not to try.

The average credit card interest rate was as high as 23.1% in June 2018 and the average household credit card debt is £2,613. Credit card providers know that interest rates are one of the most important things to customers, and they get you hooked using that 0% introductory rate in the hopes you'll forget about when it ends. It's never been easier to switch. Most providers now give you access to free credit card eligibility checkers which give you the chance of being accepted before actually applying and they don't leave a mark on your credit file. If you're paying a rate of 23.1% interest on the average credit card amount, you'll save over £600 in a year by getting yourself a 0% card.

Yearly Saving: £604

Remortgage

If you own your own house this could make the biggest single impact to your cash situation. If you're one of the two million homeowners currently on your lenders standard variable rate mortgages, the best thing you can do to free up cash is to remortgage. Banks have slashed fixed mortgage rates for new customers, but when your introductory deal finishes, you automatically move onto the standard variable rate and prices of these haven't reduced at all. The average mortgage rate for someone with a 25% deposit on an amount of £150,000 is about 4.75%. This would mean paying roughly £850 a month. If this was similar to your mortgage and you switched to one of the current best two-year deals of 1.49%, you would save a massive £250 a month. You can compare mortgage deals just like credit cards and insurance these days on the internet so there's no real effort involved. Most companies will also cover all the solicitor's fees for the process too.

Yearly Saving: £3,000

Switch Bank Accounts

British banks are still scrambling to win new customers ever since the war between switching perks started. At the time of writing, the bank which pays the most is HSBC advance, which gives you £150 up front. There are lots of other banks with similar offers if you search on the internet. The best thing of all is the switching service requires no hassle from you as it's all done by your bank. We've recently used the switching service and there were no problems at all. Everything was changed automatically! The banks also liable for any charges that might happen because of missed payments and redirecting any payments from your old account so it really is free money to put to work investing.

Yearly Saving: £150

Agreements to not splash on gifts

This one's becoming more popular and it can save tonnes of cash, especially for big families. Do you have many friends or extended family that you give gifts to? If not, great. If you do, I'm sure you know it's easy to spend a lot of money on birthdays and holidays. Spend just £35 per gift, twice a year for six loved ones and you're looking at £420 per year. It's easier than you think to come to an arrangement with friends and family that means you're avoiding a lot of costs. We use this tactic as a family. We used to spend a fortune on gifts for extended family, but eventually, we decided it was too much and something needed to be done about it. Beth's one of six siblings, so with birthdays and Christmas it could mean buying up to 10 gifts a year just for her siblings– never mind the niece and nephews, parents, friends, kids of friends, and then my side of the family! There's an agreement in place whereby all Beth's siblings "buddy up" and so everyone buys a gift for somebody different. Birthdays get an obligatory nod of acknowledgment but no presents. We only focus on our own family and children now, which has massively cut down the cost.

Yearly Saving: £420

Do a direct debit detox

The average British person wastes around £40 of direct-debit spending every month for products or services that aren't used or are forgotten about. Make sure you're cancelling as many as you can as soon as possible after you've stopped using them! The most common things not used or considered "expendable" are gym memberships, cinema card fees and museum memberships but there are many others. Sense check your finances against this list and make sure you're not paying out for any of these if you're not using them:

- Unused subscription TV channels (e.g. premium sports/film packages for Sky/Virgin)
- Unused streaming TV services (Netflix/Amazon Prime)
- Unread magazine subscriptions
- Old dating site memberships
- Unused packaged bank accounts (the ones that charge a monthly fee)
- Unused club memberships
- Insurance for things you no longer have – This is a big one!
- Unwanted charity direct debits

Yearly Saving: £480

Don't buy bottled water

Whilst the water out of your tap obviously isn't "free", it may as well be when you compare it to the crazy price per unit of bottled water. A reasonably cheap 500ml of bottled water is about 50p on the high street. If you buy one of these every day, you'll pay £182 a year. Tap water on the other hand is insanely cheap in comparison. 1 cubic metre of water is 1000 litres. Severn Trent water charges about £1.40 per 1000 litres of water, which is 0.14p per litre. To put it another way, a 50p bottle of water is 71,328% more expensive than tap water! That's not a typo.... Crazy isn't it? Why would you ever buy bottled again? It's expensive and the plastic is terrible for the environment.

Yearly Saving: £182

Keep your car tyres correctly inflated

Easy to overlook but also super easy to fix. Not keeping on top of your car tyre pressure can make your car's fuel consumption worse. A drop of 15psi in your tyre pressure can affect fuel consumption by 3%. While that's a fairly big reduction in pressure, if your tyres stay underinflated for a long time and you use a tank of fuel a week to work and back – approximately

£55 worth of fuel – you could save up to £85 over a year. Even if your tyres aren't that drastically deflated, your tyres are also going to need changing sooner, and tyre manufacturer Michelin has done some testing that show a tyre underinflated by 20% will shorten it's life by 20%, meaning paying for new ones sooner than needed.

Yearly Saving: £86

Plan meals ahead

By spending an hour at the beginning of the week doing a meal plan, you can save both time and money as well as having more control over the food your family is eating. We plan our family meals from Monday to Sunday. Don't just randomly buy food in bulk with the hope of saving money though. Make sure it's what you *need*. Some things you might save on the unit cost by a few pence if you buy a bigger box/package/roll, but if you have a family, chances are that you have enough stuff taking up space in your house already. Some things it makes sense to buy bigger packets of non-fresh items, things such as pasta and rice can be quite a bit cheaper and come in pack sizes that are manageable, but speaking from past experience, any "buy-one-get-one-free" (BOGOF) deals on fresh food will often go to waste as you end up binning the "free" one because it isn't eaten in time. Then again, you can still buy fresh food in bulk if you cook it and freeze it. The freezer is your friend, so have your meal plan, but maybe allow some room for adaptation to the supermarket offers.

The UK Office of National Statistics says that the average weekly UK spend on food is £59. As a family of 4, we've managed to get it down to about £40 with some crafty planning and no real loss of nice food. There are tonnes of resources on the web. A very good book to read is Cooking on a Bootstrap by Jack Monroe.

Yearly Saving: £988

Bait and switch brands

As well as planning meals ahead, swapping some branded for non-branded can be easy. I'm not saying go out and fill your cupboards with everything dented, wonky or past its sell-by-date, but tactically switching stuff that isn't even obvious when switched is the best. Kids can be fussy little things. If it's not the "right" type of cereal or bread it can be a hard time getting them to accept something new. We've swapped our branded Cheerios at a cost of £2.45 a box to supermarket own-brand at a cost of £1.25 a box – for the same size box too. In the cupboard, we have those re-sealable plastic cereal containers which means that when they're refilled after the shop, you throw the cereal box in the recycling and hey presto, no evidence of the switch and the kids can't even tell the difference! This is just one example, there are lots of other things you can try this with to free up even more cash.

Yearly Saving: £62

Do activities instead of going shopping for fun

While there's no "average" for this as every family is different, consider doing some fun, free activities instead of just going out into your town centre to have a mooch around. Don't make *shopping* the activity in itself. You'll often end up buying things you don't particularly want or need. How far is the nearest park? Is there a lake or some fields nearby? Do you and your family ride bikes? Do you have a garden and enjoy gardening? What sports do you like? There are absolutely loads of things to do which don't cost anything, or very little and which are easily available.

Your local council website may have some schemes or guidance, and apps such as Hoop can provide you with details of age appropriate activities in your areas. Some will obviously cost money, but you can apply filters to weed out all the free ones. As a bonus, these sorts of activities will get you and your family out and about socialising and generally being more active.

Adding it all up

The grand total of all of the savings listed above means you could save thousands and none of the things I listed means significantly changing your lifestyle either. Freeing up cash to invest is vital in forming the basis of your financial future. Even if you're not in a position to do everything, there's almost certainly something on your list that can give you a regular cash boost. As you'll find out later in the book, you really don't need much money to start!

If you want to take things to the next level, the MSE Money Makeover tool is here: https://www.moneysavingexpert.com/family/money-help/. This takes you through everything in detail and enable you to give your finances a full makeover. It includes many other tips I haven't been able to list in this section and links to other resources to take it as far as you want to take it. Good luck freeing up that cash!

Grand Total Saving: £7,547

7 INVESTMENT ENCYCLOPAEDIA

There's so much information available on the internet about investing, but for a novice or someone starting out, it's often overwhelming. There's just too much. More information doesn't mean better decisions, and can actually make your decisions worse. I've thought carefully about what to include in this section to make sure you can focus on the things you definitely need to know first. There are some basic topics and some more advanced. You don't need to be an expert when you start investing, but you do need to know how to make informed choices based on your personal circumstances and this is the knowledge I hope you'll gain in this section.

This chapter explores the core set of things you need to know to be a good D.I.Y investor. I'll explore the main investment types that you could be holding in your overall investment portfolio and indicate my perceived risk about each of them. I'll also explain what types of investments I think you should avoid completely and some principles you need to be aware of to make you a better investor. If you have some investment knowledge already, this section might be covering old ground at some points but I'm confident there's something in this chapter for everyone.

Compound Interest – start as early as possible

Albert Einstein is often quoted as saying compound interest is the most powerful force in the universe. He probably didn't ever say that, seems like a bit of a random comment from a physicist, but either way, the power of compound interest is extraordinary.

Compound interest is literally interest that is earned on your interest. Every time you earn interest, it's rolled up – compounded – into your original investment, meaning that as the years go by, at the same time your pot is growing, the interest on that pot is also growing, which means your money grows faster and faster and so on. It's completely free money. The effect is made even more powerful with regular investment contributions. Time is the key to big gains when compounding. The longer you compound, the better the result as we'll see below.

Let's go through what happens to your money when you *don't* compound the interest first. This type of interest is called "simple" interest. Imagine you had inherited some money and decided to invest it tomorrow. You put £10,000 away for a hypothetical 10% return each year for the next decade, hoping to put this cash towards the kid's university fees or a deposit on a house. As you can see in Table 8, 10% of £10,000 is £1,000, so you earn that each year for 10 years, with total interest of £10,000 - simple.

Year	Money you're earning interest on	Interest	Total Returns
1	£10,000	£1,000	£11,000
2	£10,000	£1,000	£12,000
3	£10,000	£1,000	£13,000
4	£10,000	£1,000	£14,000
5	£10,000	£1,000	£15,000
6	£10,000	£1,000	£16,000
7	£10,000	£1,000	£17,000
8	£10,000	£1,000	£18,000
9	£10,000	£1,000	£19,000
10	£10,000	£1,000	£20,000
	Total Interest	**£10,000**	

Table 8

With compound interest, each year's interest payment is compounded into the amount that you earn interest on for the following year. In Table 9, as you're taking advantage of the compounding effect, the amount you earn interest on increases each year when your previous years interest gets added onto it. So, for example in year 2, instead of it just being 10% of £10,000 like it was with simple interest, compound interest adds on your first year's interest. This turns it into 10% of £11,000 = £1,100. This effect means that every year, your pot grows at an even faster rate as the new interest is added on. Over the course of 10 years, in this simple example compound interest means you end up with over 50% more money without any additional contributions at all.

Year	Money you're earning interest on	Interest	Total Returns
1	£10,000	£1,000	£11,000
2	£11,000	£1,100	£12,100
3	£12,100	£1,210	£13,310
4	£13,310	£1,331	£14,641
5	£14,641	£1,464	£16,105
6	£16,105	£1,611	£17,716
7	£17,716	£1,772	£19,487
8	£19,487	£1,949	£21,436
9	£21,436	£2,144	£23,579
10	£23,579	£2,358	£25,937
	Total interest	**£15,937**	

Table 9

When saving for 10 years beats saving for 30

Longer term, the effects are even more extraordinary. Let's look at another example. Suppose you're 30 years old, and you decide to start investing regularly. You set aside £200 a month and invest that every month from now on until you're 60. We'll assume you earn 7% a year on average, which is entirely possible over the long-term. After 30 years diligently paying into your investment pot, you check your account to see whether you've saved up enough money for early retirement. You find yourself with a value of £242,575 as shown in Figure 4. That's not bad at all!

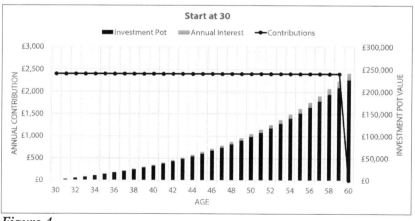

Figure 4

Now let's assume in an alternate reality you'd decided to start investing sooner at 20 and invested your £200 per month until you were 30. When you turned 30 you decided to stop your monthly contributions. You figured it was sensible to leave your 10-years' worth of investments as a nest-egg and not touch it until you're 60. You end up with £27,500 *more* money at £270,087. Compound interest is so powerful, that as you can see in Figure 5, your 10 years contributions beat your 30 years of contributions purely because of the time that your money is invested for.

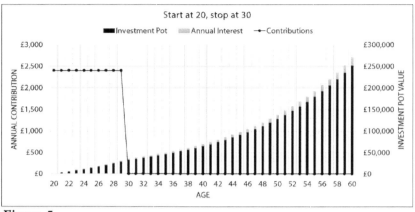

Figure 5

£24,000 (invested from 20 – 30 years old, then left alone until 60) beats £72,000 (invested from 30 – 60 years old) because of the effects of compound interest. You pay 3 times as much but lose out because you missed out on that first 10 years' worth of compounded returns. Time invested is so incredibly powerful. The end result of not starting early means you miss out on that all-important growth. It's crazy.

To apply the concept of compound interest to your investments, you *must* be re-investing any income you earn from your investments otherwise you miss out on the benefits.

Pound-cost averaging

You could call pound-cost averaging a cousin of compound interest. Both concepts involve long-term investing and both can help maximise the value of your investment pot over time. It's also the main way I want to encourage would-be investors to start their investment journey. Trying to "time" the buying of your investments at the lows and then sell at the highs is a problem for any investor regardless of the size of the investment or where the money is invested. Some of the best-known fund managers and investors in the world think it's almost impossible to time the markets properly.

Pound-cost averaging translates to a "little and often" style of investing. If you want to invest £1200 in shares of a company, rather than buying it all in one go, you would split it out over a long period of time, e.g. £100 worth of shares each month for a year. The price of the shares you're buying is changing constantly. Share prices change by the minute based on the information available in the market. News reports for example can have a big effect on share price. Just this week writing this chapter, online fashion retailer ASOS told investors it had seen a "significant deterioration" in trading conditions and that full year sales are now only expected to rise 15% compared to the previous guidance of 20-25%. This caused a 40% crash in the share price. Whilst it might ring alarm bells in investors' minds that sales are *only* rising by 15%, this hasn't put off the CEO and chairman from buying more shares in the company this week, hoping to take account of pound-cost-averaging and also indicating they're confident about the future of the company. You buy more shares when prices are low and less when prices are high, which means you're averaging the cost of your purchases over time. You end up "smoothing out" the cost.

Pound-cost averaging isn't just about the average price, it's also about establishing discipline, creating a habit and avoiding emotional action. If you have a lump sum of cash and decide to put 100% on one stock or fund, you could be buying just before a big spike in the price, which is great, but you could just as likely be buying before a big drop in price too. You can easily sabotage your own investment journey with this technique. Pound cost averaging does away with that feeling of thinking "*Have I picked the right time to buy?*" because you're regularly making lots of smaller purchases, you're not too concerned with short-term price movements. You can also automate this process to make it even more hassle-free.

Pound-cost averaging goes hand-in-hand with how most people, including me, fund their investments, which is through the monthly earnings from work. Investments can be set up to come out of your account on payday, with the bills, but nothing like a bill as instead of paying someone else, you're paying *yourself* with investments. In the same way a snowball continuously grows in size as it rolls down a mountain, your investments have the ability to make money, and then make more money from that money, so on and so forth. The key is to just start.

Here's an example of how pound-cost averaging affects how much you pay for shares:

Lump sum Leonard decided to invest £10,000 and buys 1000 shares valued at £10 each. Regular investment Roger also has £10,000 to invest and decides to buy £5,000 worth of the same shares split across two months. The first month's purchase means he buys 500 shares, (£5000/£10), but in the second month, the share price reduces to £9.50. This means the second months purchase buys him 526 shares

(£5000/£9.50). For Roger, rather than the full £10,000 being affected by the drop in the share price, only half his money drops in value because he split his purchases over the 2 months.

Regular investments every month have this same effect, as the share price will change randomly throughout every day of the year depending on who's buying and selling, so in months where the share price is low, you're just getting extra shares for your money. Overall, if you've invested in the company for the right reasons, over the long term this will help with your returns. It also helps you to develop the right behaviours to consistently invest and is less of a gamble than investing it all at once. Pound cost averaging will mean you'll avoid that sense of regret had you invested a lump sum before a big market drop.

Pound-cost averaging works well as your investment knowledge increases over time. You start off contributing to some assets, then as you learn more, form your own opinions, likes and dislikes about particular companies, you can bend and flex your regular investments based on their performance or your newly acquired knowledge. You might learn more about emerging markets, suppose you see greater opportunities with smaller companies overseas than UK-based "blue chip" investments. Your investments are much more agile unlike big lumps of cash.

The main disadvantage is that over time, if prices continue to rise – which obviously everyone wants – you'll increase the average cost at which you buy your shares. In reality, nobody has perfect information about how prices will change, but pound-cost averaging is still best-placed to take advantage of any volatility in the market. Provided you're investing in a company for the right reasons, it should offer the best value for money over the long-term.

Competitive Advantage

Competitive advantages are unique traits and features of a company and its products that are seen by customers as setting them apart from the competition. This is looking beyond the pound signs and a bit deeper into the non-physical things the business has to offer. It's often the reason behind brand loyalty and why you prefer one product over another. You look at that company as having a competitive advantage over others. It's also one of the things would-be investors in a company should be looking for although they might not be obvious at first-glance. When deciding whether or not to invest in any company, you need to ask yourself the following questions:

1. What sets this company apart from other companies in the same market?
2. How do they take advantage of their position in the market to provide the best service/products to customers?

There are three forms of generic competitive advantage, developed by Michael Porter of Harvard University back in the 1980s.

Cost Leadership Advantage

This is probably the most obvious competitive advantage in business. If a business can sell a product or service that's a lower cost than other competitors, this gives them a cost leadership advantage. Similarly, if a business can produce those products at the *same* quality for less than their competitors, this is even better. A business with cost leadership advantage generally has a streamlined process, with strict efficiency and takes advantage of bulk/wholesale pricing. With a focus on slim profit margins, they must scale their sales to give larger profits. This means big volumes and lots of customers. Therefore, lower costs naturally result in higher profits and the company can add value to the customer by giving some of that cost benefit to them. Look out for businesses that may have recently invested in improved production facilities. Does a business have noticeably cheaper products compared to the nearest direct competitors? Think along the line of IKEA, Aldi and Lidl.

Differential Advantage

A differential advantage is where a business' products or services set it apart from the competition due to unique benefits or characteristics. Google's search algorithm that powers it's search engine is an example of a differential advantage. They formulated a different way of displaying the relevant information where someone typed in a search term which was much better than their competitors. This set them apart from everyone else.

This type of advantage also allows companies to charge a premium for products or services where they're recognisably better than the competition. This should mean an increase in profits and better overall business performance. The differential advantage could be several things, such as more expertise, better facilities, friendlier staff, more pleasant buying facilities. Airlines are a good example of this, if you ask customers to rank airlines in terms of preference, most airlines are assumed to be equally safe, so many people look at on-board services to differentiate between airline options. When investing, see what a company does differently to its competitors and whether or not it's working to attract more customers.

Focus Advantage

A focus advantage means actively targeting a smaller (niche) customer base rather than trying to target everyone. This strategy is often used by smaller businesses because they don't have the resources or size to target everyone. The idea is to focus on the needs of a small number of customers. This smaller focus means that within this smaller group of customers, overall customer satisfaction is much higher. Electric car maker Tesla is an example of focus strategy. Tesla decided to break into the electric vehicle market with a luxury sports model in 2008. At the time, the electric vehicle market prioritised economy rather than form and function. Tesla decided not to compete with the more generic electric car models like the Toyota hybrids and instead go for the smaller, but high-end market where they could charge a price premium – and they make some pretty fantastic cars if you haven't seen them already.

Small, medium or large companies?

One of the key decisions when it comes to investing – mainly applicable to shares – is whether or not to go for small, medium or large companies. Whilst I've over-simplified that massively, the basic concept is true, as different size companies have different advantages and disadvantages. Company sizes are based on the market capitalisation of a company, which is its overall value. The greater the value, the larger the capitalisation, or "cap". In the UK, large-cap companies are generally considered to be the ones that are listed in the FTSE 100 index. Mid-cap companies are generally considered to be those listed in the FTSE 250 index, where the market cap is about £4 billion down to £500 million. The FTSE Small Cap index includes, you've guessed it, the small-cap shares worth as "little" as £150 million. Shares with a market cap of less than £150 million are usually found on the Alternative Investment Market (AIM). These are known informally as micro-cap companies.

Large cap

These are the big, heavy behemoths of the business world. They're the juggernauts and some of the largest companies in the world. They tend to be multi-national companies with operations in many different countries. They're very often household names with easily recognisable logos and are very popular amongst investors. Their size means they get a lot of attention and are frequently included in news stories. Examples include BP, Shell, Tesco, McDonalds, Coca Cola and Apple.

The size of these companies means they don't usually grow rapidly because it takes a lot of time and resources. The share prices of these companies are usually less volatile and more likely to pay dividends (see the next section for information on dividends) to investors. There's a lot of information and research about large-caps. The downside is there are often lots of conflicting opinions from different analysts because large-caps are so popular.

Large-caps are likely to trade at or around what's called "fair value". This is a concept whereby all the information that could influence a share price is considered to be "in the price". This means that there's so much news and analyst coverage, all the information that can affect a share price is known to virtually every interest party, so it's highly likely the current share price is an appropriate value. As such, you'd expect less surprises from large-cap companies, but just because of their size, it doesn't mean they're always a safe bet. They're slow to react to change, so if for example some legislation comes along that affects a business's operation, or their customers quickly go out of favour with their product, it can be bad news to a company of this size.

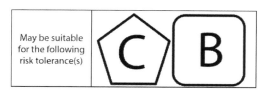

Mid cap

Mid-cap companies usually have better growth prospects than large-caps because they're smaller. These types of companies could be considered the "sweet spot" of the investment landscape. They're usually large enough to have experienced management teams, their distribution network is good, and they have a strong presence in the market. They can grow their profits at a faster rate than large-caps because there's more "room" in the market to grow into and they also benefit from less bureaucracy and less layers of management. Mid-cap companies can also be the target for mergers and takeovers by the large-caps, which can boost investment returns. Just recently, this happened with GlaxoSmithKline and Pfizer. These two pharmaceutical powerhouses recently announced plans to merge their customer healthcare businesses in a new world-leading joint venture.

Mid-caps are more sensitive to investors speculating on the price which means there is usually more volatility. This can be good though because you have a better chance of buying shares at a "discount". As there is less information for mid-cap shares than large-caps, it's more likely that this isn't reflected in the price, so you can buy shares at a good price easier than you could with a large-cap.

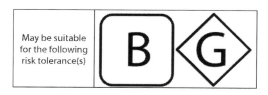

Small cap

Small-caps can deliver some of the highest returns over the long term, but you need to be prepared to deal with a lot of volatility and a higher chance of failure. These companies are less known than their bigger brothers which means there's a lot more room for growth.

There's often less interest and less analysts covering the day-to-day activities, so there's potentially a lot of information not in the price of the shares. This is a direct contrast to the large-cap companies, which have too much news and analyst coverage. Sometimes being hidden from the public eye can mean great investment opportunities lie waiting to be found, just because nobody knows about them.

Small-cap companies also have better integration with the board of directors. The board members will often own large parts of the company, which acts as big incentive to make sure the business performs well, which is a big contrast to the bigger companies that have boards of directors paid giant sums of money irrespective of how their business performs.

May be suitable for the following risk tolerance(s)

Does the company pay a dividend?

A dividend is the term used to describe the pay-out of a chunk of the company's earnings to shareholders and it's one of the main ways an investor gets a return from buying shares. Dividends usually come as cash payments but can also be paid in shares. They are paid at fixed intervals, usually quarterly or annually and this varies by the companies that pay them. The amount also varies and depends on the share price and company earnings. No company is obliged to pay a dividend. The decision whether or not to issue a dividend comes from the company's board of directors. If profits aren't paid out to shareholders via dividends, they're kept within the company as retained earnings and reinvested for growth.

The term "dividend yield" is used to describe how much money you're getting from a dividend-paying company and effectively acts as the interest rate paid to you for owning them. It's the rate of income you receive from owning shares. It's usually expressed as a percentage of the share price or "pounds per share". For example, at the time of writing, Aviva shares currently cost £3.94. They have a dividend yield of 6.92%, which works out to a dividend of about 27p per share. If I owned 100 shares of Aviva, my dividend pay-out would be about £27.

Start-up companies and high-growth companies very rarely offer dividends. These types of companies are more likely to report losses in their early years and any profits that are made are reinvested to keep growing the company. Dividends usually come from established businesses with more predictable profits. Casting your mind back to the previous section, mid-caps and large-caps are the main payers of dividends. They issue dividends to maximise the returns for their shareholders because they're already big and can't grow as fast as the small-caps can.

There are also certain industries that pay out bigger dividends than others. Oil and gas, financial, pharmaceutical and utilities companies often aim at paying out dividends to their shareholders, which reflects the sizes of these types of companies – they're often very big, react slowly to changing market conditions and so need to keep their shareholders happy.

Naturally, investors too often focus on the shares that pay the highest dividends. While a high-yielding dividend is great as you're getting a bigger percentage of the business' profits, it's not the only thing to look out for.

The first thing to look for is consistent profits. If a company isn't steadily profitable, forget about it, as if you're interested in dividend shares, the payment is likely to vary and could stop completely. Look for long-term earnings growth expectations between 5 and 15%. Any higher growth expectations than 15% are just as bad because it often results in disappointment when companies fail to achieve this level, so the share price suffers, and inevitably so does the following years dividend payment. Also look for companies that have consistently increased their dividends for several years in a row. This increases the odds of continued dividend growth. There are even a select few companies commonly called the "Dividend Aristocrats" that have consistently increased their annual dividend payments for over 25 years! These include companies such as Diageo, City of London Investment Trust, Spirax-Sarco Engineering and Caledonia Investments.

The Pay-out Ratio is another way of assessing the quality of dividend-paying companies. It's a measure of the percentage of profits a company pays out. It's calculated by dividing the company's current annual dividend rate by its last 12 months' worth of earnings. This gives you a clue about the sustainability of the dividend. Higher pay-out ratios, especially ratios above 1 are a warning sign and are likely a sign that a cut to the dividend rate is due in the near future. As a general guide, the average pay-out-ratio for FTSE All-share companies (the biggest companies in the UK) for the 2017-2018 financial year was 0.54.

If the dividend stock offers a high yield, consistent profits *and* a low pay-out-ratio, these shares stand a much better chance of offering a high *total* return to your money over time. This is because your dividend payments add extra money to the shares if they grow in value, which in turn buys more shares, that pay more dividends, and so on, through the power of compounding. Dividend paying shares can form a good part of your portfolio provided you reinvest the dividends. Unless you have a good reason to take the money as income, you should absolutely be reinvesting any dividends earned into buying more shares.

All about bonds

You can buy bonds directly as they are issued from the UK governments Debt Management Office but most bonds are traded on the stock market.

A bond will have what's called a "face value" (often referred to as par value or nominal value). Effectively this is the value of the fixed portion of debt that's being offered out as a loan. It's also the amount of money that the bond issuer promises to repay the bondholder at the maturity date of the bond. Typically, each bonds face value is £100 in the UK. Due to how bonds work, a bond with a £100 face value won't necessarily be trading for £100…

Bonds can trade at a "discount" or a "premium" compared to their face value depending on general interest rates and how credit-worthy the bond issuer is deemed to be. As market interest rates change, a bond's interest rate (coupon rate – which remember is fixed) will either become more or less desirable to investors. This will influence the price they're willing to pay. Let's work through an example.

A conventional UK bond will be written to look like this: - "Treasury stock 6% 2020". This means that a £100 gilt would pay you a 6% coupon (£6 a year) until your initial £100 loan is repaid in 2020. After evaluating your alternatives, you decide that this is a pretty good deal, so you buy this bond at its face value. Now let's suppose that next year, interest rates in general go up. If new bonds from other companies with a £100 face value are now paying an 8% coupon, buyers won't want to pay the £100 face value for your 6% UK Government gilt because any returns they would earn are less than they can get from these newer 8% bonds from other companies. If you wanted to sell your bond, you'd have to offer your bond at a discount so you might have to sell it for £95. This works the same if interest rates go down. Your bond, if you chose to sell it, would be worth more than £100 and would be priced at a premium. You might be able to sell it for £110 since it would carry a better rate of return than what was available on the market or with similar bonds.

Whether you buy a bond at a discount or a premium doesn't affect the value that's paid to you on maturity. If you spend £95 or £110 on your Treasury Stock 6% 2020, the value paid at maturity is always the face value of the bond, so in this case £100. When you're buying bonds, the cheaper you buy them compared to their face value, the more profit you'll make.

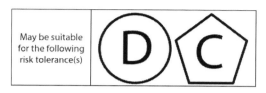

May be suitable for the following risk tolerance(s)

Bond Credit Ratings

Just like you and me, a government or company has a credit rating. The rating of a bond gives the potential bond purchaser some insight as to how risky the loan is. The risk of being unable to pay back loans, or "defaulting" as it's known, influences the overall interest rate of the bond. Riskier ratings often lead to higher interest rates and higher returns but also higher likelihood of not getting your money back. Two companies, Moody's Investors Service and Standard & Poor's, carry out roughly 80% of the global credit ratings, which includes bonds. The ratings you'll come across can be summarised in Table 10 below.

Rating	Riskiness
AAA	Highest quality, lowest likelihood of default
AA	High quality, very low likelihood of default
A	Strong, low likelihood of default
BBB	Medium grade, medium likelihood of default
BB, B	Speculative, high risk of default
CCC, CC, C	Highly speculative, high risk of default
D	Default, unable to pay back debt

Table 10

A bond is considered "investment grade" if its credit rating is BBB and above. What this means is that these bonds come from financially robust businesses such as governments and utility companies. Bonds are considered "high yield" or the not-so-affectionate term "junk bonds" if they are rated below BBB. These are bonds from companies that are at a high risk of being unable to pay their debts. In order to get people to invest in their bonds, they offer higher rates of interest to tempt them to loan out their money.

My thoughts on bonds are that they're mediocre at best. They're good low-risk investments, especially gilts, as it's considered very unlikely for the UK government to default on its debts. There's a lot less choice in bonds and no way to take advantage of the growth of the company. Bonds can play a part in your portfolio to balance out your overall risk, but they're unlikely to transform your family's wealth. Give them some consideration in your portfolio but don't focus on them unless your appetite for risk is low.

Don't get confused about Premium Bonds

I'm only really including this as a discussion so you don't confuse normal bonds with premium bonds. Premium bonds are one of the most common "investments" in the UK although you're not actually investing your money in an asset that's going to increase in value. The best way to describe them is a combination of saving (but without any interest) whilst playing the lottery. That might sound like a bit of fun, but you earn absolutely no extra money whatsoever unless you win a prize. Premium bond numbers are drawn every month at random, so it isn't really investing. As we discussed earlier, as the years go by, inflation will slowly reduce your money over time, so if you regularly buy a lot of premium bonds, that money will be worth less and less unless you keep on winning prizes. I don't recommend premium bonds – I think there are much better ways to put your money to work.

Funds – what they are and why you need them

Funds are one of my favourite investments and make up a major part of my portfolio. They act as a "basket" for other asset classes, so when you buy units of a fund, you can buy many different assets in one go without the hassle of individually picking them. Think of funds like chocolate selection boxes. You buy a box and you have a mixture of different things all inside it. There are a lot of different choices you can make with funds and you'll find them out as you read on.

The way they work is that a fund pools together the money of lots of different investors and then invests that money on their behalf. The manager of the fund will then invest in different types of assets such as shares, bonds and property. This automatically spreads your risk with very little work required on your part.

Funds are mainly categorised by sector or industry. Sector funds focus on different geographic sectors such as UK, US, Global, Europe and Asia. A fund specialising in the UK will only have UK shares, bonds or property within the fund basket. Funds can also be divided by industry type, such as mining, technology, pharmaceutical or financial services. Funds aren't just limited to being sector or industry specific though, they come in all shapes and sizes and there are loads to choose from.

If there's a popular selection of companies that fits a particular theme, chances are there is a fund somewhere created for investors to buy if they want. Have a search on the internet and you'll find thousands, from the straight forward to the weird. For instance, there's a fund founded in the USA called the "Vice Fund" that only owns gambling, tobacco, weapons and alcohol companies! Here's an example of a fund shown graphically in Figure 6. You can see how each of the asset classes makes up a different percentage of the overall fund.

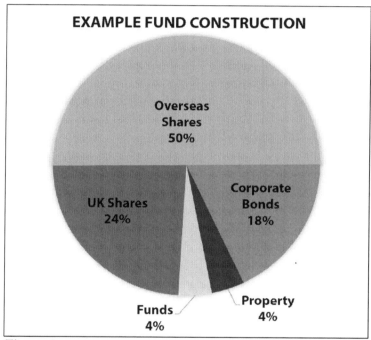

Figure 6

When you buy into a fund, you're buying things called fund units, which are tiny versions of the whole fund. So, if you spent £100 when investing in the imaginary fund in Figure 6, you would have £24 invested in UK shares, £50 invested in overseas shares, £18 invested in Corporate bonds, £4 invested in property and £4 in other funds.

Investors typically earn a return from a fund in one of three ways:

- Income is earned from dividends on shares and interest on bonds held in the fund's portfolio. A fund pays out this income it receives over the year to unit-holders in something called a "distribution".

- If the fund sells assets that have increased in price, the fund has a "capital gain" – a rise in the value of the asset resulting in a profit. This is also passed onto unit-holders of the fund with a distribution.
- If the assets in the fund increase in price, the fund's units increase in price, much like shares in a company. You're then able to sell your fund units for a profit.

Each day, usually around 12pm, the fund manager will calculate the value of the fund, giving a price per unit. Anyone wanting to buy or sell units does so at the price calculated at the valuation point. Investors need to submit their requests to buy or sell units before a price is declared, so you're not aware of the exact price you'll receive before a deal is placed. This is different from shares, as there is often a "live" price that varies throughout the day. The complexity of funds means that it's not possible to do a live fund price.

The once-a-day valuation of funds makes them great for regular investing. You're not tempted to try and "time" your buying and selling as if you were buying shares. Instead, you can invest a set amount per month into a fund, then your cash buys you as many fund units as is possible at whatever the price is on the day – this is pound-cost averaging in practice. You're just harvesting as many units as possible each month.

Unit Trusts vs OEICs

There are two main types of fund, Unit Trusts and Open-Ended Investment Companies (OEICs; pronounced "oiks"). They're very similar (and essentially provide the same product to the end investor) but it's worth highlighting some of the main practical differences.

Unit Trusts are a type of "open-ended" UK investment fund. The term "open-ended" means that the fund manager can create new units of the fund to meet demand for any investors wanting to buy them. These units can be bought or sold at any time.

An OEIC is also an open-ended UK investment fund. This is the newer of the two fund structures and was introduced in 1997. Many unit trusts have converted to OEICs, which allows them to be sold in different countries across Europe but they also have better pricing structures which is the main difference between unit trusts and OEICs.

OEICs only quote a single price. You buy your OEIC funds units for the same price you sell them. Unit trusts have something called a "bid-offer spread" which separates the funds units into two prices called a "bid price" and an "offer price". Sometimes instead of bid you might see it as "Sell" and "Buy" instead of offer.

The bid price is the price you'll get when you sell your units back to the fund, hence the name – it's what the fund is willing to bid for it. The offer price is the price you'll pay to buy units in the fund and is always slightly more than the bid price. Just like when you buy foreign currency, it'll cost you more to buy it than you get when you try and sell the leftovers back after your holiday. The bid-offer spread of a unit trust allows the middle-men in the market to make a nice profit. Here's an example:

Widget Enterprises Unit Trust	
Bid/Sell: 539.24p	Offer/Buy: 544.59p

Table 11

The fantastic Widget Enterprises Unit Trust is offering its fund units to the public at the prices in Table 11. It's common practice for many UK shares and funds to be quoted in pence sterling, otherwise known as GBX.

- The bid price (the highest price I can sell them for) is 539.24p.
- The offer price (the lowest price it'll cost me to buy them) is 544.59p.
- The bid-offer spread (the difference between both) is -5.35p or 0.98%.

This means that as soon as you buy any units in this trust, you're already at a 0.98% loss. You'd need at least a 0.98% rise in price to break even. Even if you wanted to sell them back immediately after buying, the best price you'd get for them would be the bid price (the lower of the two). Different unit trusts have different bid-offer spreads, but obviously the smaller the spread, the better off you are, as the smaller the gap to close to make money.

I'm a big fan of funds, but unit trusts pricing structures bother me because I don't see a need for continuing to operate this needlessly complicated pricing structure. I find OEICs to be fairer and more transparent in their pricing with just the single charge for buying and selling.

There are some other subtle differences between unit trusts and OEICs but nothing that makes any practical impact in your investing so I won't go into them here. It's easy to research yourself if you're interested further. The bottom-line is the price between unit trusts and OEICs is different. You still get a small slice of a big pool of different types of investment whichever type of fund you pick and they're both still great investments. You can find out if a fund is an OEIC or unit trust on the details page of the fund, which can be found by a simple Google search.

Income vs Accumulation

Funds give you the option to buy in either "Income" units or "Accumulation" units. They're like two sides of the same coin. The phase of your life is going to influence what type of units you choose. If you're due to retire soon, and reading this book because you have a big pot of savings that you want to put to use, the income units are probably for you. These units pay out dividends as cash, directly into your bank or broker account, hence why they're called income units as they act as a source of income - perfect for retirement.

If you're like me and you're a long way from retirement, accumulation units are what you want. Accumulation shares automatically reinvest any dividend earnings back into the fund until you decide to cash-in – they accumulate all the dividends within the confines of the fund in order to boost the fund's overall value. Accumulation units are for long-term growth and I currently have several accumulation funds as part of my portfolio. It automates the process completely so you aren't tempted to siphon off your earnings over time.

Let's work through a simple example. Figure 7 and Figure 8 below show how your money behaves in the different types of fund unit. Imagine there's a fantastic new fund, the Widget Enterprises Fund, that's just about to launch and is going to offer accumulation units and income units for £5 each. You decide to buy one of each unit. A year passes by and the fund's assets pay out a pretty generous dividend of 10% because of the good performance of some of the companies in the fund.

The income and accumulation versions of the fund are due the exact same dividend, but each will treat your 50p dividend differently. Figure 7 shows that for your income unit, you've still got one income unit worth £5 and the dividend of 50p is cash paid straight into your investment account. This can be withdrawn, reinvested or simply held in your account. There's no change in value to your original £5 income unit though because all of your gain is transferred out of the fund.

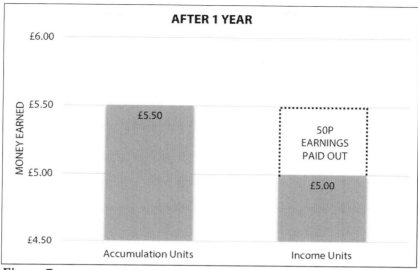

Figure 7

Your accumulation unit on the other hand, is now worth £5.50 if you wanted to sell it. You've earned the same 50p as the income unit but this is now rolled-up into the fund. As per Figure 8, your number of units remains the same, but the process of the dividends being rolled-up into the fund increases the value of *every accumulation unit* held by every investor of the fund.

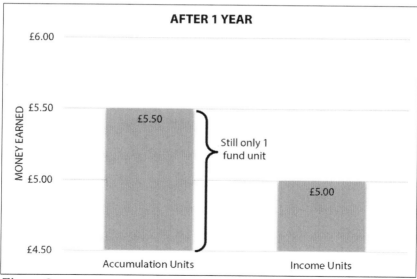

Figure 8

Over any given single year for a fund, the performance of the income and the accumulation units is identical. They're still the same fund with the same investments after all. But after that year, the differences paths of income and accumulation units start to show. With income units, you have a steady stream of income every year, but it's withdrawn from the fund for you to do as you please. With accumulation units, you benefit from compound interest as the dividends are rolled up into the fund each year. With income units because your gains are being paid out, you're keeping the amount you earn interest on every year the same, which over time reduces the total amount of money you get because you're no longer earning interest on interest. Just as an example in Figure 9, if you bought and kept 1 unit of this imaginary fund for 20 years, you'd earn £14.50 with income units but over double with accumulation units.

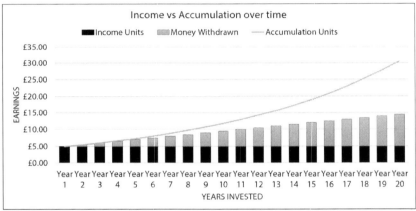

Figure 9

One inconvenience to accumulation units is you don't see the physical cash get deposited into your account, so it can be a bit demotivating if you're the type of person that needs that constant incentive to keep investing, but you can take comfort in the fact that your money is continually and automatically getting reinvested to maximise your earnings over the long term.

There's nothing stopping you from re-investing cash from your income units into the same or a different fund, but beware of the costs of this. Most investment providers have "reinvestment charges" for cash from income units, but not on accumulation units. This will eat into your returns. For instance, some brokers charge a 1% dealing commission of any income reinvestment – there's more on charges later in the book. All of my own fund units are accumulation and they're perfect for my circumstances.

Passive funds vs Actively managed funds

Yet another choice to make with funds is whether or not to go passive or active. Broadly speaking, a fund can be managed actively or passively. Actively managed funds are run by professional investment research teams and fund managers. They make all of the decisions about what the market or sector the fund should focus on, what assets are going in the fund and when to buy or sell them. They have widespread access to lots of sources of information across the world. Reps from these teams will also make personal visits to companies of interest to decide whether or not to invest in them.

The basic goal for actively managed funds is to beat the market. Fund managers try to either create a return that's better than the market as a whole or protect your money and lose less value if the market falls. There's the potential to make much higher returns than the general market if your fund manager makes the right decisions but it can also go the other way too and you could lose less than you otherwise would have if they pick the wrong investments. This can appeal to a lot of investors as you have someone tactically managing your money when picking and choosing assets. For example, if the fund has a global focus, if a particular world market starts to suffer, a fund manager would try and reduce the amount of assets from that particular region by selling them and buying some from elsewhere that has better prospects.

Passive funds (sometimes called "index", "index tracker" funds) are still run professionally but they don't have investment research teams and fund managers picking the assets to include in the fund. There's no fund manager making any "active" decisions about what to buy and sell. Instead, they track a stock market index in order to try and mimic that market's performance. Remember from earlier in the book, a stock market index is a measurement of a part of the market and there is at least one index for each market around the world. It's a tool used by investors to describe a market and to compare investments in it.

There is still a big, ongoing debate about the benefits of actively managed funds versus passively managed. Cost wise you may be looking at a management fee as a percentage in the region of 0.1% for a passively managed fund or 1% for an actively managed fund for example. As you're paying more for actively managed, you'd expect the performance to be better, but, that's not quite true. There's a lot of research to show that professional fund managers' active trading consistently under-performs the market as a whole.

A study from American financial services company "Standard & Poor's" showed that a massive 74% of actively managed U.S funds underperformed the market from 2009-2012. Very few actively managed funds can consistently stay at the top. Out of the 703 funds that were in the top quarter of performance in 2011, less than 5% of those funds managed to stay there until 2013. There is however something to be said about active management and its ability to protect against market downturns. Over the past 20 years, the top 25% of active fund managers outperformed the market in the years when the market performance was negative, showing that there may be some benefits in fund managers protecting your money.

In short, active funds try and beat the market with the expertise of the fund managers, passive funds try and own the market and ride on the gains by minimising costs and owning a little piece of everything. I'm not against active fund management, but it's difficult to do successfully for the long term. Whilst passive management isn't a guarantee for success, it keeps costs low meaning you keep more of the returns.

Partial vs full replication funds

With a tracker fund you're owning a small representation of the whole market that the fund is tracking. The tracker funds goal is to make sure it's the closest representation possible to whatever index it's tracking. There are two ways of getting this done, "full replication" and "partial replication".

A fund using full replication distributes all its holdings proportionately alongside the index. For example, a tracker fund tracking the FTSE 100 will buy shares in all 100 companies in the index, in the same proportions as those companies make up the index. This is called their "index weight". As of June 2018, the index weight of Barclays as a portion of the FTSE 100 was 1.63%, so a full replication fund tracking the FTSE 100 would also have Barclays shares making up 1.63% of that overall fund. Here's the concept shown visually in Figure 10. This tiny imaginary market has 10 companies, Company A to Company J. They have a total value of £10,000. A tracker fund uses full replication to split the fund with the same percentages as the top 10 companies in the market, so Company A is 13% of both the market and the tracker fund, Company B is 5% of the market and the tracker fund and so on.

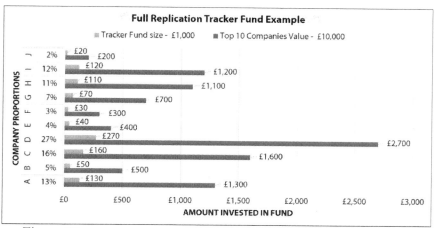

Figure 10

Partial replication funds are different in that they buy a sample of the index. This method is generally used when it's too hard to buy all the shares in an index. An example is the MSCI World Index tracker fund. This tracks over 1600 companies from 23 countries, so it would take a crazy amount of effort, time and cost to hold all of the shares of the companies in that fund. Instead of doing this, partial replication of all those companies is achieved by weighting using *sectors* instead. For example, the MSCI World Index tracker fund currently has 12.74% of the fund focusing on health care. There are too many individual health care companies out there to buy their individual shares, but so long as the total amount of investments in the fund are made up of 12.74% of companies in the health care sector, any companies can be picked.

<u>Fund classes</u>

A fund can have more than one "class". Different classes in a fund represent the different units the fund manager has created to suit certain types of buyers, for example institutional investors such as pension funds. Each unit in the fund may have different costs and minimum investment levels. This can affect the performance of a particular class of the fund and is therefore reflected in the different pricing.

A different class may also indicate whether it is an income paying unit or an accumulation unit. Each of these classes may have a different price to reflect the differences in their charging structure and the way they treat income received from the fund's underlying holdings. There is no pattern across fund groups, Class A for one fund isn't necessarily the same as Class A for another fund. 'A' is simply used to differentiate the fund from another unit of the same fund, class B or class Z for example.

As an individual investor there is little point of worrying about the different fund classes. You're not getting a different product with different classes, each class of a fund has the same selection of investments, so it hasn't got a big real-world impact. Focus on the goals over the overall fund itself and when you've found the right fund, all it really boils down to in my opinion is which class has the lowest costs.

Exchange Traded Funds (ETFs)

ETFs are effectively a hybrid share and fund. Like funds they are made up of groups of different assets as per Figure 6, but unlike funds and as the name suggests, they are traded on the stock market exchanges like regular shares. Think of them like tradable packages of funds because they have many of the same properties as regular funds.

Most but not all ETFs operate like index tracker funds, so they cover a whole market. Buying an ETF unit, you get very wide exposure to a lot of different assets just as you would a fund. They can be bought and sold throughout the day and aren't just valued once-per-day like regular funds. ETFs also have two prices - the bid-offer spread, like unit trusts. Some also have full and some have partial replication like tracker funds discussed in the previous section.

Regular trading of ETFs means paying regular dealing charges. Dealing charges on shares are often much more expensive than dealing on funds so there's not really much advantage with an ETF unless you are trading frequently – and you shouldn't be trading frequently if you're following the principles in this book!

Many resources recommend ETFs because with a low product fee, the physical ETF can be cheap, but factoring in dealing commissions you then start to really eat into your gains, especially regularly investing. For the long-term wealth-building investor, I don't think they have much use. The nature of the makeup of ETFs are complex and can be higher risk than their regular fund counterparts. As far as my opinion goes, they don't offer any advantages over regular funds, so I don't recommend these for new investors unless you have a specific interest in them.

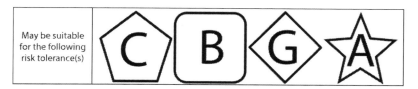

Crowdfunding is the future of lending

Crowdfunding is starting to take the world by storm, as a credible alternative to high street lending and borrowing. It's not an asset class in its own right, but it's a new way of investing that may appeal to investors that have higher tolerances to risk. Crowdfunding is a process whereby many people, the "crowd", contribute a portion of money to invest in either the debt or equity of businesses. Many of these businesses are start-ups and some are established companies looking for more funding to expand their operations without having to approach a bank or the stock market.

This is great news for helping British businesses. Small and medium sized companies are the main driver for Britain's economic growth, but they often struggle to borrow money from high street banks. Crowdfunding supports their needs for expansion by using the general public to raise cash instead.

The other benefit to crowdfunding is that it's unlocked a previously hidden area of investing. Only wealthy investors and businesses used to be able to invest in start-ups, but crowdfunding has made it so everyone can get involved. Crowdfunding takes place with the help of specialist companies that act as facilitators for these businesses. They usually take a slice of the pie in return for offering out these investments.

Debt Crowdfunding/ Peer-2-Peer Lending

Debt crowdfunding is also known as Peer-2-Peer (P2P) lending and the more widespread of the two types of crowdfunding. There's big money and fast growth in P2P lending right now. The UK's P2P market grew from £300 million in 2011 to £4.6 billion in 2016. The industry became regulated by the Financial Conduct Authority in 2014 offering better protection for investors. P2P lending matches up investors who are willing to lend money with borrowers – either individual borrowers or small businesses looking for loans. You earn money by the borrower paying you back interest on the original amount you loaned out. You can earn anywhere between 2% - 12% interest depending on the specific investment options and providers you go with.

Traditionally, people and small businesses who wanted a loan would usually apply for one through the bank. The bank would run wide-ranging financial checks on the applicant's credit history to determine if they would qualify for a loan. If the answer was a yes, the interest rate would vary depending on the banks interpretation of their credit risk. With P2P lending, borrowers take loans from individual investors who are willing to lend against a pre-agreed interest rate. There is no big corporate banking middle-man so borrowers can get better rates when borrowing and investors can get higher interest rates than if the money was just sat in a bank account.

There are still credit-checks involved for borrowers and many P2P lenders have their own credit-worthiness tests on top of that to protect investors, but on the whole, it is easier to obtain a P2P loan than via a high-street bank. This is because individual investors are prepared to take on more smaller risks than large financial institutions are willing to take fewer big risks.

My favourite P2P platforms are shown in Table 12, but there are many more out there than that. These companies connect lenders to borrowers through their websites. They take care of all the arranging of the loans and collecting money from the borrowers and charge a fee for this service. You're effectively acting as "the bank" to a borrower.

As with any investment there are risks. By being directly connected to someone who's borrowing your money, there is a risk that if a borrower fails to repay (known as "defaulting") then you could lose all of your money. Most of the main P2P platforms recognise this and have different ways of protecting your money.

Crowd2Fund loans are typically secured against business assets or director guarantees. This is an agreement that means that if the business can't pay it back, the directors have agreed they're personally liable to repay it.

RateSetter has something called a "provision fund" which covers any borrowers defaults. If you lend money via RateSetter and the person who borrows your money can't pay it back, RateSetter will pay it out of their own pocket from their provision fund instead and they currently have a 100% track record of doing this. It's still not a guarantee as there's a risk if the provision fund runs dry you won't get your money back but it's a very good way of them looking out for their customers.

WiseAlpha doesn't have any fund or guarantee. It tries to protect against defaults by offering senior secured loans and bonds, which have first priority for payback in case of any problems. It also offers bonds from established companies, many of which are household names, such as Virgin Media and British Gas. If a borrower fails to pay back money owed, WiseAlpha will act on behalf of all investors in negotiations to recover the money owed, but at least for the larger companies, the risk is much lower than lending to individual borrowers.

Zopa splits your money into £10 chunks to across lots of different borrowers to lower your risk. The minimum money you can invest in Zopa is £1000, which means that no one person would have more than 1% of your overall investment.

Funding Circle was the first company to use P2P lending in the UK back in 2010 so they have a lot of experience. They also recently went public on the London Stock Exchange, so you can even invest in shares of Funding Circle itself as well as using its services! Your money is lent to small and medium British businesses, so it's great to support the backbone of the British economy. Like Zopa though, the high initial investment of £1000 is off-putting, especially if you're looking to invest regularly. There's also no provision fund, so much like Zopa, you're encouraged to split your money in small chunks between different businesses.

Company	What are you investing in?	Minimum Investment	Potential Max Return per year
Crowd2fund	Business loans	£10	8.7%
Ratesetter	Individual loans	£10	6.3%
WiseAlpha	Business loans and bonds	£100	16.5%
Zopa	Individual Loans	£1,000	5.2%
Funding Circle	Business Loans	£1,000	6%

Table 12

Out of all of these P2P platforms, in my view RateSetter comes out on top. It has a very low minimum investment amount, which is great for getting started and also for experimenting with how you like their service. The provision fund is a great confidence-builder for would-be investors. RateSetter also offers rolling and fixed-term investments. You can have a monthly rolling contribution you can withdraw at any time, but you can also lock in your money for 1 year or 5 years at a better rate of interest. You also don't have to physically pick who to invest in, as RateSetter takes care of all of that for you. Finally, for even easier investing, it's integrated with a fantastic app called Plum – discussed in the Digital Investment Helper section – which means it can make investing a breeze and is currently our main P2P platform we invest in.

Equity Crowdfunding

Instead of investing in debt, as in P2P lending, you can invest in equity/shares and become part-owner in the business. Equity crowdfunding is the process of exchanging money for shares in a business that isn't yet listed on a major stock exchange. These are the main types of businesses that are looking to be financed via crowdfunding as they can't approach traditional lenders easily. The main ways to make a profit when investing in a company via crowdfunding are:

- Being bought-out by another business – The company you've invested in is sold to another company for a cash lump sum, which is divided between shareholders and your shares are bought from you for more than you paid for them, generating you a profit.
- Initial Public Offering – The company decides that it's time to list on a stock exchange, then shareholders can sell their shares at the price determined by public demand.

Equity crowdfunding is inherently riskier than debt crowdfunding as if you invest in an unestablished business or start-up, you risk losing all of your money if the business fails. There aren't any "provision funds" or anything like that because you're ultimately owning an asset – and if the value of the business falls to zero, so does your investment. There's nothing to bail you out. The reward however can be much greater than P2P lending because there's no fixed interest rate and the company's share price gains are effectively uncapped – they've all got unlimited potential.

As well as share price gains, because you own equity/shares in the company, there's also the prospect of the company paying out dividends. This is highly unusual for companies that are crowdfunding as they want every penny spare re-invested to grow the business and generate profits, but depending on how well they perform over the years this is a possibility further down the line. To be clear though, don't expect a dividend in the short-term from any crowdfunding investments. With equity crowdfunding it's all about growth, growth and growth.

Another thing about equity crowdfunding is don't expect to be able to sell your investments in the short-term. Equity crowdfunding is definitely a long term, 5+ years investment in almost all cases. Most of the companies raising money via crowdfunding aren't currently making any money, they aren't publicly traded on a stock exchange and there aren't a steady stream of buyers and sellers. They often have their years of growth and profitability ahead of them, so it's about using the tools in this book on top of your own research to find a company you really, truly believe has the potential to make it big. The idea then is you get in at the early stages as an investor, and watch your investments grow over the years.

There are two main players that offer equity crowdfunding in the UK, Crowdcube and Seedrs. Both offer a similar service. There's a notable difference between the fees of both platforms. Crowdcube currently charges 1.5% of the amount you've invested up front. Seedrs on the other hand doesn't charge you up front to invest, but if and when the business you've invested in makes a profit, you're charged 7.5% on any profit made.

Both Seedrs and Crowdcube have what's called a "Secondary Market" where for a fee, you can get rid of your shares of companies when you want, but there's no real benefit to this. It's more of a trade for your original cash back, you won't see a good return on your money from using the secondary market feature. Do your due diligence up-front and stay committed or don't invest at all.

Equity crowdfunding is highly speculative. These are often companies that have no proven track record, and an uncertain future, but with uncertainty, there is opportunity. You should only be allocating a small portion of your overall portfolio to equity crowdfunding unless you have a really high appetite for risk and make sure you're comfortable being invested in that company for the long term.

How to invest in property

You don't need to buy houses to get some good exposure to property. This section is nothing about actually buying physical property, but these are the main ways to get exposure to property without having to buy entire buildings. Property investing is traditionally seen as safe by many people and while this isn't strictly true as there are risks in property just like any other investments, there's often an air of comfort surrounding bricks and mortar. It might give some security to those who think there's opportunity for the property market in the future.

Real Estate Investment Trusts (REITs)

A REIT is a property investment company. It gives you indirect exposure to the property market, in the way that you're not physically buying buildings, instead you're buying shares in a company that buys buildings. They're newer in the UK than other parts of the world. Popular in America, REITs began to appear around 2007 in the UK. A REIT can be easily traded on the stock exchange exactly the same as any other share. To be considered a REIT, at least 75% of the company's profits must come from property rental and 75% of the company's assets have to be in the property rental business. To encourage investment in UK property, REITs don't have to pay corporation tax or capital gains tax on their investments. They also have to pay out 90% of their rental income to investors, which is a good, steady way to get some dividend payments. This can mean better gains for you as an investor. Most of the returns from REITs are from the rents paid by tenants on the buildings it owns.

The issue with this is that because REITs pay out almost all of their income to investors, this leaves little for them to reinvest in new properties. It may mean they have to resort to selling new shares or borrowing extra money. You need to watch out for debt, and the loan-to-value (LTV) ratio. You might be familiar with this concept from your own mortgage. A higher LTV means more debt is being used to finance a property purchase. An LTV of 50% means 50% of the purchase is funded by a loan. As we've all experienced over the last several years, property prices can be very volatile, values can change quickly and REITs that use higher levels of debt to fund their property portfolio expansion might find themselves in trouble fast if a downturn hits rental income.

Evaluating REITs comes in two parts – dividends (just like some shares pay), and changes in Net Asset Value (NAV). NAV represents the value of all of the assets owned by the REIT, so it considers all the property value minus the value of its debts. This figure is then divided amongst the shares in issue to get the "NAV per share". For example, let's assume a REIT has £1m worth of assets and £500,000 worth of debt. There are 1 million shares in issue. The end result is (£1,000,000 – £500,000)/1,000,000 shares.

The NAV per share is £0.50.

If the value of the properties in the REITs portfolio increase, the NAV will grow, which is an indicator of the strength of the underlying property held by the REIT. If a REIT is popular, for instance if it owns assets in a trendy sector, the share price would trade at a premium, above its NAV. The same is also true for when a REIT isn't performing so well. As a general rule, the REIT share price and REIT will tend to move together.

An example of a popular REIT is Tritax Big Box. This REIT buys and rents out giant warehouses which are at the centre of modern e-commerce logistics and shipping services. These warehouses have automated handling equipment that keeps stock flowing as efficiently as possible. Suitable sites of theirs are large and ideally cover 45,000 square metres or more near to major motorways. These types of sites are limited in supply and critical to most big business' infrastructure which means there's less chance of their properties not having paying tenants.

Most of their clients are big businesses on long leases and upward-only rental reviews which fund future income growth. Tritax's business is really quite simple. Buy and rent out giant boxes for businesses to store their goods in. Their debt is reasonably low to limit the LTV risks discussed previously. With average interest rates of less than 2.4%, using some amount of borrowing to part-fund purchases where the typical starting yield is 5.7% is a great way for them to expand. Tritax has also raised more cash for investments through rights issues - where shareholders are invited to increase their holding. Given the ever-increasing growth of online retailers, demand for this type of property should remain good for the future, so Tritax seems in a fantastic position to take advantage of that to try and provide good returns for its shareholders. REITs are my favourite way to invest in property due to some of the problems facing property funds as you'll see when you read on.

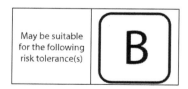

Property funds

Property funds operate exactly the same as a normal funds. Most property funds only deal in commercial properties which means offices, retail spaces or industrial sites. As of 1st of September 2018, the property investment tools in the UK changed. The Investment Association "Direct Property" designation was created to show you which funds invest in physical buildings and a second sector, "Property Other" designates funds that invest overseas or in the shares of property companies, which at least clarifies what you're investing in.

Unlike regular funds, direct property funds are not such a good way to invest in property, as such I think they're a different level of risk. While it might sound appealing to own bricks and mortar, especially through the convenience of a fund, the way these funds are run can be problematic. The first is that commercial property is not easily or quickly bought and sold. It takes a lot of time, labour and is expensive. This means that fund managers have problems. As an investor you obviously want to put a lot of money into funds which have good performance and a positive outlook. But it can take months to find and buy suitable commercial properties and these funds can end up holding a lot of cash, which means missing out on rising property prices in the process and affecting investors overall returns.

Secondly, when the forecast isn't so good with property or off the back of poor investing, investors in property funds want to sell their units. This means that fund managers are forced to sell properties in order to give investors their money back who are cashing in. The properties that are the quickest and easiest to sell are often the best properties in the fund, so this "short-termism" from needing cash to fund the investors selling up is at the detriment of the remaining investors as they're left with the worse investments.

In extreme circumstances, property funds can even stop you selling your fund units completely for a period of time. In 2016, in the wake of the EU referendum, several high-profile property funds were forced to stop withdrawals as people predicted the value of their investments would hit the floor when Britain left the EU. This influx of withdrawals meant that the major property funds didn't physically have enough cash available to meet investor demand for the ones that were selling up, so they were forced to stop sales completely for a period of time. Be cautious if you want to invest in property funds.

Cryptocurrency, the next asset class?

As I write this, something crazy is happening. There is a lot of hype and mania surrounding cryptocurrency. You might have already heard of the world's most famous cryptocurrency, Bitcoin, you might have no clue what I'm talking about, but we're witnessing the creation of an entirely new digital-only asset class. If you have a very high tolerance to risk, this could be a fantastic opportunity or an overhyped disaster. Many people from the old school financial elite are sceptical. Nobel Prize-winning economist Joseph Stigltiz's view is that it should be outlawed. Others are optimistic, Bill Gates, co-founder of Microsoft said:

"Bitcoin is better than currency"

Regardless of the views the financial elite have, cryptocurrency is gaining serious mainstream attention. Many of the general public aren't even aware of the existence of cryptocurrency and yet the market capitalisation (the number in circulation multiplied by the unit price), just for the most popular cryptocurrency Bitcoin, has increased from approximately £30 million in 2012 to £87.5 billion in 2018. That's an increase of 291,566%! There are hundreds more cryptocurrencies and these impossibly-high gains have caught millions of investors' attention.

You might be wondering what cryptocurrency actually is but I'm not here to give you a lecture on this topic just a crash course so you know enough to be informed. Let me be clear up front though – this is for **speculative investors only**. It's without a doubt one of the riskiest and most volatile investments you can make. You need to be prepared to lose all of your money if you invest in cryptocurrency. If in doubt, definitely don't invest.

<u>What is it?</u>

Cryptocurrencies are digital currencies, like a form of digital cash in the form of exchanges of computer data. Not just a digital representation of a currency but an actual currency in electronic form. Today, credit card companies and banks act as the "holder" for a lot of your money. A bank will have a database holding information about you and your money and this can be a target for hackers. Cryptocurrencies don't need any central authority and so aren't exposed to these types of hacks. Most cryptocurrencies also share a common commitment to decentralisation, which means not being controlled by any single government, being guarded from political manipulation and control. A way of looking at cryptocurrency is that cryptocurrencies basically represent the electronic version of a "cash-in-hand" transaction. There's no middle-man involved, nobody to trust to exchange your money on your behalf, it's straight from you to whoever you're giving money to, but instead of handing them a note or some coins, you're sending them some data.

Just like real money, cryptocurrencies are often referred to as "coins" and are also stored in digital "wallets". These wallets are protected by a key, an extremely complicated password that you and only you know about. Just like real money, you can buy products and services with cryptocurrencies too. You still have full control over your payments like any normal currency and as cryptocurrencies slowly start moving towards being accepted around the world, bigger businesses are offering them as payment. Current business accepting cryptocurrency include Microsoft, Subway and Expedia.

How does cryptocurrency work?

I'm not going into too much detail here, there's plenty more information available on the internet, but you need to know the basics to help you understand what you're investing in should you want to get involved. Cryptocurrencies were developed on top of an invention known as "blockchain", which has many other applications other than digital currencies. Currency is just one of hundreds of applications that use blockchain technology. Sally Davies, Financial Times Technology Reporter put it best as:

> *"Blockchain is to Bitcoin, what the internet is to email. A big electronic system, on top of which you can build applications. Currency is just one."*

A blockchain is a digital public ledger (a recording of transactions) that keeps track of digital currency transactions without a central database. All of the participants in the transactions hold the entire ledger of all the transactions, which is permanent, unalterable and continuously updated as more transactions are made. The ledger is like "The Matrix". It's everywhere in the cryptocurrency network but you can't see it directly. The authenticity of the ledger can be verified by the entire community, which means nobody can control or tamper with a cryptocurrency directly.

How to invest and buy

Under no circumstances should you confuse buying-and-holding cryptocurrency as an asset, with active trading of cryptocurrency. The only way I'd even consider you invested in cryptocurrency if you were interested is to buy-and-hold and that's the approach I'm taking with my small holding. There are adverts littered over the internet for all types of cryptocurrency trading websites for the "active" trading of cryptocurrencies, but this is almost certain to lose you money in the long term.

When I say "buy cryptocurrency" this means that you end up with effectively a digital product in your cryptocurrency wallet. You don't own shares, it's not part of a fund, it's not like a bond. Out of all the traditional asset classes, it's the most similar to a commodity. There's no interest to be earned, there's no dividend paid or no coupon paid. They rely on perceived value, a bit like a precious metal, so any real-world money to be made from cryptocurrency should be in the form of capital gains - buying at a low price and selling at a high price.

What's interesting about cryptocurrency is that it was created with the idea that it would replace "real-world" money as currency, and we'd all be paying for our shopping in Bitcoins. Due to the speculative nature of the technology, naturally this had everybody interested. When there's interest, there's attention, when there's attention, there's demand and when there's demand, the price increases. The "currency" aspect of cryptocurrency is really the secondary use for the technology at this point in time, because the cryptocurrencies themselves have become valuable to hold just by people predicting they'll be big in future.

As with any investment, taking a long-term approach is essential, but even more so with cryptocurrency. There are lots of cryptocurrencies out there and the only real thing that sets them apart is intrinsic value. Intrinsic value, when applied to the concept of a normal business, can be defined as the value of all aspects of the business, both physical and non-physical. This includes things such as the physical assets of the business such as cash, property and machinery, but also the non-physical aspects like demand for the product or service, the belief in the leadership team, the size of the community and partnerships.

Given that most cryptocurrencies are nothing more than a digital idea or concept and have quite limited real-world use, determining intrinsic value for cryptocurrencies is almost impossible. The factors mentioned above might give some indication of the value of the cryptocurrency but then there's always the irrational/emotional factors that end up distorting the facts. For example, does the cryptocurrency with the highest price – Bitcoin – have the most intrinsic value out of all other cryptocurrencies? Probably not, but a lot of investors think it does and hence why it's the highest priced of them all.

Types of cryptocurrencies

Just like any business you might invest in, there are very good and very bad cryptocurrencies. There are so many in fact, an entire website deadcoins.com was set up to catalogue the ones that have failed. The list runs into the thousands of failed projects, many of which of which were scams.

Despite all of this, and seeing the potential it has in the future, it definitely has some of my interest, but only makes up a tiny portion of the family portfolio. Out of all the investment classes in this book, cryptocurrency is definitely the least "normal", but could turn out to be the most interesting. Some information about the biggest and most-traded cryptocurrencies are in Table 13.

Cryptocurrency	Discussion
Bitcoin	The original cryptocurrency Bitcoin is the market leader and has an established reputation worldwide. It has a large community base interested in it. It's received the most media attention of all the cryptocurrencies so far and is the most widely known by the general public.
Ethereum	Bitcoin was originally designed purely as a digital currency/cash substitute system, but Ethereum was designed to help businesses use blockchain technology for different applications. The underlying currency on the Ethereum network is called Ether. Ethereum is a multi-use technology and supports business applications for online gambling, social media platforms and financial exchanges. There are hundreds more applications in development.
XRP	"XRP" is the name of the digital currency that facilitates payments on the Ripple network. Ripple is an American technology company that developed the Ripple network. The name "Ripple" is often used interchangeably with XRP but don't confuse the two. They exist independently. They are however still linked. Ripple owns about 60 billion XRP to facilitate payments on its network. If more providers join Ripple's payment network, demand could increase and so could the value of XRP.
Litecoin	Litecoin was released in 2012 and is often seen as the "silver to Bitcoin's gold". Litecoin is based on a global payment network that is not controlled by any central authority. It's a form of digital currency that is like Bitcoin in many ways but supports transactions about four times faster.

Table 13

The strangest thing about cryptocurrency is that you can mine it. Mining cryptocurrency is painstaking, but it's enough that you're aware that it exists, because mining is effectively "minting" digital coins, which can affect the value of certain cryptocurrencies. One of the reasons some cryptocurrencies hold intrinsic value is because of their limited supply. Once a certain number of coins have been created, that's it, there can be no more new coins at that point. Bitcoin has a limit of 21 million coins, Litecoin has a maximum of 84 million coins. Mining cryptocurrency in volumes that generate a meaningful return is difficult now. In the earlier days, it was possible to do this easily with relatively easy-to-get hardware, but the concept of mining provides diminishing returns. As more coins are mined, the rewards get smaller, meaning you need more computer power, and therefore more expenses. Now it's primarily done on an industrial scale.

It's possible to buy cryptocurrency with just your debit card on a centralised cryptocurrency exchange. There's plenty out there on the internet, just make sure you triple check the legitimacy of where you're buying from. We spent an evening or 25 scouring the internet for these and reading up on the different platforms. Scams and poor customer service make this an extra barrier to investing in cryptocurrency, so make sure you look for multiple reviews.

What is an Initial Coin Offering (ICO)?

Another section I'm including only to warn to stay away from. If you're researching cryptocurrencies, you might come across various ICOs. Stay away from ICOs. An ICO is where a company markets a new currency with various promises of future performance in order to raise a lot of money to put those promises into action. This term has been borrowed from an "IPO", which stands for Initial Public Offering and is the way in which a business moves from being privately owned to being publicly owned on the stock market. That's where the similarity ends. IPOs are heavily regulated and normal businesses need to jump through multiple regulatory hoops. ICOs are completely unregulated, filled with hype and are often scams. The perfect combination for parting a fool and their money. A recent study showed that more than 80% of ICOs conducted in 2017 were confirmed scams, with $1.34 billion lost to scammers.

Established cryptocurrencies are already high risk and hard to value given the nature of the industry, but most at least serve some purpose in some industry somewhere. Now imagine how hard it is to value an ICO with what is often a completely new company, with no track record, a new mysterious concept for a digital product, with no clear route of return on your investment. At that point everything is almost 100% guesswork. You might as well visit a casino. If you do choose to invest in cryptocurrency, stay far away from any kind of ICO.

Commodities

Did you know you can profit from putting the food on your table? One of the very first of the traded assets, people have traded commodities for thousands of years. Commodity investing is focused on raw materials that are either used directly, such as food products, or used as building blocks to create other products. Commodities are divided into four main groups – precious metals, energy products, industrial metals and agricultural products. Agricultural commodities are also known as "soft" commodities as they are grown rather than mined, and include items such as coffee, wheat, cocoa beans and sugar.

Commodities show "low correlation" with shares, which means that the factors which might affect share prices are not going to affect commodities in the same way. They can be a good addition to your portfolio to adjust your risk. That being said however, the issue is that commodities are usually a lot more volatile in their prices than shares, so are considered riskier.

As commodities deal with real-world consumption of physical barrels of oil, bushels of wheat, tonnes of sugar etc, the supply and demand dynamics can make the price of them change very quickly. The price of Brent crude oil, an international benchmark, was being sold for $115 a barrel in June 2014. By January 2016, the price had plummeted to less than $30 a barrel because of big increases in production from oil-producing countries which drove the price lower around the world. Big harvest of crops usually creates the same effect, as there's more supply than demand, but bad weather can do the opposite and prices can soar if harvests don't produce as much as expected. There's a lot of unknowns.

Precious metals such as gold are often considered as a safety net asset and store of value. Back in June 2016, when it was announced that the UK had voted in favour of Brexit, the price of gold had its biggest jump since the financial crisis of 2008 because of all the uncertainty.

There are three main ways to invest in commodities.

- Buy them directly
- Buy shares in commodity companies
- Buy through pooled investments such as funds.

The first is obviously the simplest way. If you want to invest in gold for example, there's nothing stopping you from going out and buying gold bullion bars or coins from a jeweller. There are firms that offer buying services online, they just require an internet search. You can get coins and bars delivered to your doorstep. The problem with this is that you're probably going to be buying small quantities of precious metals unless you have a big safe somewhere in your house. This means that you're not going to get a very good price per unit of weight, plus it's still an expensive business even in small quantities. At the time of writing, a 100-gram gold bar currently costs just over £3000.

Buying shares in commodity companies is a good way to get indirect exposure to the commodities. Much like property as discussed earlier, you don't end up owning the physical commodities yourself but you're then profiting off the back of the profits the company makes when it mines/grows them. BP and Royal Dutch Shell you've probably heard of as famous oil-mining companies, so to get exposure to oil you can buy shares in them. Both of these companies also happen to pay dividends. Glencore is another company that focuses on metals, minerals, energy and agricultural products, which can give you exposure to those other commodities.

An investment in a commodity fund is an excellent and easy way to get exposure to commodities. Much like "normal" funds that hold a selection of assets of a similar theme, commodity funds function in the same way. There can be a bit more choice with commodity funds though. You can have a fund that holds the physical commodity itself, e.g. a fund that holds a large amount of gold bullion, or you can have a fund that invests in companies that are involved in commodity-related fields like miners, agricultural businesses and oil drilling.

May be suitable for the following risk tolerance(s)

Contracts-for-difference (CFDs) and spread-betting

I've only included this section so that you stay away from these. Several years ago, one of my first and failed ventures was with CFDs. I started sensibly with a tracker fund, but then decided to turn up the risk level too much. I was seduced by the amazing potential returns and I ended up quickly losing money because I didn't know what I was doing. Had I known what I know now about CFDs, I would have never even tried it. Luckily, it was only a small amount of money I experimented with and now you're able to benefit from my initial mistake. The only reason I'm including a section on this topic is to persuade you to keep far away from it.

CFDs and spread bets allow investors to gain exposure to the price movement of a big range of assets without actually owning the asset, or putting up the full value of those assets. Rather than profit from the long-term increase in value of an asset by buying and holding it, you're trying to profit from very short-term changes in price and then re-sell it for a quick gain. If that sounds like an easy way to make money, it's an even easier way to lose it - by the bucket load. CFDs and spread bets are both what's called "leveraged" products. Being a leveraged product means that your *losses* are amplified as well as the gains. The way a lot of accounts are set up, there's no safety net to hit, even when you've lost everything. You can end up losing significantly more money than your original deposit if something goes seriously wrong, meaning you can end up actually owing money to the company.

The not-so-hidden-truth about leveraged products

The main problem with a short-term trading style using leveraged products is that market fluctuations in price over the short timescales of these trades are often extremely volatile. In simple words, lots of people lose lots of money very often. There is no reliable way to accurately and consistently predict short-term price movements like this and this has been researched thoroughly before and there is a theory called the Random Walk theory. Random Walk theory states that changes in share prices are independent of each other and therefore can't be used to predict the future movement of the price. It's the main reason why you see the phrase "past performance is not a reliable indicator of future performance" when looking at most financial products. It's because nobody can truly predict what's going to happen and the Financial Conduct Authority wants all investors to know that.

Nothing about the long-term value of the shares influences the price over the short-term. Short term trading attempts to spot patterns in share price data, but the long-term trends of a company, the way its products are likely to change society, or the value it can create over the long-term can't be seen in this type of trading. It is effectively just trying to spot patterns in the "noise" of random price movements.

The Financial Conduct Authority analysed a sample of UK accounts from CFD firms and found that an astonishing 82% of these accounts lose money, with an average loss of £2,200. If you're really unlucky, you could end up like Irish supply teacher Mr. O'Comartuin back in 2015. This unfortunate soul, who only earned £17,800 a year, suddenly faced a loss of almost £280,000 thanks to the Swiss National Bank lifting the Swiss Franc's price ceiling against the euro. This sent the value of the franc surging, and hundreds of people like Mr. O'Comartuin faced staggering losses.

Don't get suckered in. The only winners in this game are the middle-men trading platforms that charge you a commission. For the vast majority of people, CFDs and spread bets will not build long-term, life-changing wealth with minimal involvement. Trading platforms that facilitate these types of leveraged trades are so inadequate at boosting individual investor's finances that they're now required to display how many people lose money by using their service on their banner adverts. If you do an internet search for an investment-related topic after reading this book, you might see a targeted advert from one of these trading platforms and at the very bottom in tiny print, you'll see a warning which states what percentage of its customers lose money when trading CFDs with that provider. It's often over 75% of customers.

The techniques in my book focus on you building long-term value. Leveraged products just leads to panic, buying at highs, selling at lows and being out of pocket in most cases. I'm refusing to even give them a risk rating the risk is that high. Avoid them.

8 TYPES OF INVESTMENT WRAPPERS

N ow that you know a bit more about investing and what's involved with the various asset classes, it's time to understand the ways in which you can buy and hold any assets you plan on buying. This section goes through some of those products and services. Most conventional investments need to be kept in some form of account. If you're buying shares, funds or bonds for example, you'll need an account from a provider that can be the holder for those assets. Much like regular bank accounts, there are many providers. I'll talk about some of the best ones. Pretty much all investment wrappers come with some sort of cost. For the full details of all of the costs of the products mentioned in this section, see the chapter on costs later in this book.

Fund Supermarkets

Nothing to do with food or traditional supermarkets, fund supermarkets are investment providers that allow investors to buy, sell and hold a range of investments from different management companies together in one "wrapper". Despite being called "fund" supermarkets, many let you hold shares, investment trusts and ETFs too. They often provide a lot of research and information on each of these investments, including which industries the company or fund covers, historical and recent performance figures and information about the investing styles of each manager associated with the investment. The main point of these platforms is that they are designed for people – like you - who are making their own investment decisions. This type of service is referred to as "execution-only" as while they might have information available, they often won't give you financial advice unless you pay for it specifically.

Execution-only services are described by the Financial Conduct Authority as a "transaction executed by a firm upon the specific instructions of a client where the firm does not give advice on investments". This means you're wholly responsible for picking and buying your investments and the fund supermarket won't tell you which investments to pick.

You can hold your investments within an Individual Savings Account (ISA), a Personal Pension or a general investment account. A general investment account is the least useful of all these options as this doesn't come with any tax benefits whatsoever. The only real reason to pick a general investment account from a fund supermarket website is if you're fortunate enough to have maxed out your ISA allowance and still want to invest more money.

There are low cost fund supermarkets and premium ones. Premium platforms tend to offer more investment research so that you can base your decisions on this research and often include example portfolios, suggestions and analysis tools. Low-cost fund supermarkets operate a "no frills" approach and just offer a means of buying, selling and holding assets.

ISA variants

ISAs are the bread and butter of money storage for most of Britain. If you don't have one, chances are you know what one is unless you've been living under a rock. You might be less familiar with some of the newer ISA variants though, but they're very important in wealth generation for one major thing – saving tax. Each flavour of ISA comes with its own advantages but the basic principle is the same in all of them - tax-free money for life. Many people associate ISAs with banks however you can open up an ISA through many other companies. Many of the fund supermarkets offer ISA versions of their accounts and I've included a list of them later in the book. Any company offering an ISA must also be regulated, so don't assume your money is any safer in a bank. Your high street bank probably isn't the best place to create your ISA.

Each year, you have a maximum limit to the amount of money you can deposit across all your ISAs. You can own multiple types of ISA, but they can't exceed the yearly limit. Currently this is a limit of £20,000 for the 2018/2019 tax year. Once the year is over though, any unused allowance can't be rolled over and you lose it forever, so it's important to try and shelter as much money and investments in an ISA as possible to reap the rewards without having to pay tax. You need to save or invest before the 5th of April for it to count for that tax year. You might not be fortunate enough to max out your allowance each year, but it's good practice to put as much as you can into it as over time you can build a giant pot of tax-free investments.

The ISA allowance changes annually and there are no rules to how much you can deposit at one time. You can do it by a single lump sum, or daily/weekly/monthly contributions, whatever you feel like. The £20,000 allowance can be shared between different types of ISA. For example, you could have £2000 in a Cash ISA, £10,000 in a stocks and shares ISA, £6,000 in an Innovative Finance ISA (IFISA) and £4,000 in a Lifetime ISA (LISA). The only restrictions are that a LISA can only have a maximum of £4,000 of the £20,000 total in it and a Junior ISA (JISA) has its own separate allowance of £4,260. You'll find out what all these different variants of ISA are as you read through this chapter.

For invested money, the allowance doesn't include any interest/gains you receive in your ISA; it's strictly just the deposit amount you make. So, if you buy a mixture of investments which costs the maximum £20,000 and they happen to increase in value that same year, not only is that fantastic investing, that's completely fine from an ISA perspective.

You can't add to previous years' ISA allowances, but as long as that money stays in the ISA after the year is up, earnings stay tax free for life. For example, if you can invest £100 a month in a stocks and shares ISA, after one year you'll have £1,200 invested. When your ISA allowance resets, you add to your £1,200 tax free investments with another £1,200 – assuming the amount you invest stays the same. If you do this for 20 years, you'll have invested £24,000 tax-free – excluding any gains you may have made.

It doesn't matter what type of ISA you have, you're not locked-in to any particular ISA provider. You're completely free to shop around, and can transfer your existing ISA pot if you spot a better provider at some point in the future. You can then take all of your existing money along with you. Think of it a cargo train with carriages. You're the train driver in the main engine cab. Each year of ISA contributions is a different carriage full of money and each station you visit is a different ISA provider. If you want, you can connect them all up and move them along with you, or if you want to you can leave some of the carriages at those stations when your money train carries on to other providers.

Cash ISA

Your normal run-of-the-mill ISA is a tax-free savings account offered by UK banks and financially regulated institutions. They are the same as a traditional savings account but as discussed previously, there's currently a cap of £20,000 per year and there's no tax to pay on the interest you earn. Cash ISA interest rates are currently terrible, with the best easy-access cash ISA rate currently at 1.38% from Leeds Building Society. Don't bother with a cash ISA unless you're an ultra-cautious investor. The predicted inflation rate for 2018-2019 is around 2.1%, so you've actually lost money in the highest paying cash ISA.

Stocks and shares ISA

This is an absolute must-have for any investor. Despite the name of this ISA, you aren't just restricted to keeping stocks and shares in it. You can hold ETFs, funds, cash and bonds in this type of ISA. Stocks and shares ISAs are the main way to shelter your investments from tax. This includes all profits made as your assets increase in value, not just the original cost of them. Usually you'd pay tax on profits from shares, tax on interest earned from bonds and tax on dividend income if your investments were held outside of an ISA, but all UK shares are sheltered from tax when held inside a stocks and shares ISA. Following the principles of this book, the aim is to keep your investments sheltered for as long as possible until you need them. You can then take a big chunk of money through your entire life completely free of tax.

Just to be aware, most stocks and shares ISAs have virtually 0% interest payments on the cash kept in them as the intention is to use them for investments, so the stocks and shares variant of an ISA isn't a good place to keep large amounts of cash.

Junior ISA

A JISA is an ISA for your kids. Just like the adult version, this means tax free money. JISAs come in cash or stocks and shares flavours so you can buy some investments for your children on their behalf and make them investors before they even know about it! A parent or guardian needs to open the JISA on the child's behalf. All of the money or investments in the account belong to your child but they can't do anything with it until they turn 18. They can start to manage their own account from when they're 16. It's a fantastic way to give them a head start in life. Imagine being 18 and having enough to pay towards university fees or put a deposit on a house? The great thing is that friends and relatives can also deposit money into it for Christmases and birthdays like they would a bank account, so it's a great way to build up a "flying-the-nest" egg.

The one thing about a JISA is that it highlights the importance of building a good financial foundation with your children. I discuss this further in Chapter 9. Once they're 18, that's it, it's theirs and you have no say whatsoever what it's spent on. They could blow it all on a party if they wanted, it's entirely up to them.

For overall financial discipline, using a JISA for your kid's futures is better than just reserving a portion of your adult ISA as long as you're not contributing more than the JISA limit of £4,260. It also removes the temptation for you to try and access the money early. More importantly though, it means that when your child assumes control of their JISA on their 18th birthday, it stays in the tax-free ISA wrapper until it's withdrawn. If you were to put aside a portion of your own ISA allowance for your kids, when you wanted to transfer them the money at a point in the future, it means taking that cash outside your ISA wrapper and therefore it'll lose the tax-free status. There's also no automatic, legal right for your children to inherit the money from your own ISA account if you were to die, unless you've explicitly specified that in your will, so a JISA is a further safeguard for their future.

Innovative Finance ISA

As of June 2018, only a tiny 6% of brits were aware what an IFISA was, so the odds are quite high you haven't heard of them. The UK government introduced IFISAs in 2016, and a year later, almost £300 million was invested in them according to HMRC data. An IFISA allows some or all of your ISA allowance to be invested in P2P lending. This means tax-free earnings for investing up to £20,000 through P2P lenders.

Being able to protect my P2P lending returns from tax has been a great addition to my portfolio, and if your risk appetite means you're interested in P2P lending, you should definitely consider this. Remember from earlier in the book, there are two types of crowdfunding. Equity crowdfunding and P2P lending. Current government legislation means you can only use an IFISA for P2P lending and not for equity crowdfunding. The riskiness in equity crowdfunding means it has been explicitly excluded from the scope of the IFISA for now.

Lifetime ISA

LISAs are slightly different to normal ISAs in that you can receive money from the government on top of your contributions. The LISA annual contributions are capped at £4,000 a year but the UK government will add an extra 25% absolutely free to whatever you contribute that tax year, so you can get an extra £1000 every year. An instant 25% return on investment is incredible.

There are two main types of people a LISA is aimed at. First-time house buyers and those that want to supplement their retirement income. The LISA, like a normal ISA, comes in two flavours— cash or stocks and shares. If you're soon-to-be a first-time buyer, opt for the cash version so you have a fixed amount of cash to work with when buying a house. Interest rates are terrible on cash LISAs with the highest being 1.1% but you're still earning a guaranteed 25% from the UK government, so providing you're spending the money on a home soon, you should be OK.

There are a few restrictions with a LISA:

- You need to be between 18 and 39.
- The 25% government bonus is only paid on your annual contributions – this doesn't include any interest earned or any increase in share prices.
- The 25% government bonus is only paid until you're 50.
- You can't withdraw the cash without paying a withdrawal penalty of 25% unless you're a first-time house buyer or you reach 60 years of age.

Withdrawal penalties for a LISA might seem straight forward at a glance. If you get a 25% bonus then having a withdrawal penalty of 25% it seems like it'd leave you back where you started, but the penalty is on the amount *withdrawn* not the amount you contributed. Imagine you had your LISA open for 1 year and contributed the full £4,000. You then received your 25% bonus so your total pot was £5,000. The year after, you decide to close your LISA. The 25% penalty charge is now 25% of the full amount of £5,000 which is £1,250. This leaves you with £3,750 cash in hand. Compared to your original £4,000 contribution, you're left with £3,750 which is a loss of 6.25%. Think hard before doing this with a LISA and only do it if you absolutely, definitely have to.

Using a LISA to buy your first home is dependent on your circumstances. Most people aren't lucky enough to be a cash homebuyer, so you can use the LISA proceeds to put towards a mortgage on your first property – an investment in its own right. Whilst shares are the overall better performer when compared to cash, you're risking short-term market volatility if you invest in shares when you're about to plan on buying a house. You're already getting a guaranteed 25% return on any cash in the form of a bonus.

If you're putting the money away for retirement however, opt for the stocks and shares version. I hope you're reading this with more than a few years left to retire, and that I've gotten to you soon enough to make a big difference to your personal finances, in which case, there are higher rewards at stake. The government bonus of 25% effectively protects you from a 25% loss in real terms during any downsides your investments have over the years, and then bolsters your returns if your investments increase in value over the years. Both versions of LISAs are ideal if you're self-employed. Not having the buffer of a workplace pension is tough, but you can still make a very big positive impact to your future finances, and this is one of the tools you can use.

Personal Pensions (if you're self-employed)

There are about 4.8 million people in the UK who are self-employed and this number is increasing every year. According to the Money Advice Service, almost 50% of all self-employed workers between 35 and 55 have no personal pension whatsoever. That's terrifying. The longer you put off sorting your pension, the more of a shock you'll get and the bigger the financial shortfall will be in your retirement. It's time to take control.

If you're self-employed, no doubt about it, you should have a personal pension as part of your investment strategy. It's an important part of your investing journey. You're entitled to the state pension in the same way as anyone else, but as we know from earlier in the book, it's not near enough to retire comfortably on. You won't have the fortune of an employer contributing to your retirement, but you can still take advantage of free money from the government in the form of tax relief on your contributions so it's essential to put away as much as you can realistically afford. You've seen the power of compounding over time – the earlier you start the better your chances of building up as big a pot as possible for retirement.

Irregular income and no employer contributions do make it hard. I know it's not easy, it's a difficult habit to keep. You need to be disciplined. There's no one forcing you to do it or choosing a scheme for you, so this means you need to work that bit harder to keep it in control.

When it comes to picking a personal pension, it's not as hard as it sounds. There's choice in personal pensions just like there is most products. There are too many to list here, but just as you would compare a phone contract or car insurance on the internet, you can compare pension providers on comparison sites such as www.money.co.uk.

LISA or Personal Pension – which should I pick for retirement?

Both of these products are ideally suited to the self-employed and it might be a bit unclear as to which to choose in retirement. The decision depends on your circumstances. The LISA is definitely the more flexible product. If there is a real, life-changing emergency and you need the money, you have the option to withdraw your money from your LISA, although as discussed you will suffer a penalty. The problem is that this then leaves you with less money in retirement. A pension on the other hand locks your money away for you and is completely inaccessible until you want to retire but you get the bonus of tax relief on your pension contribution. For simplicity's sake, I want to compare the contributions without any investment growth added on, so it's clear what your options are.

While you make an instant 25% return on any LISA contribution, the amount you can contribute per year is hard capped at £4,000. For personal pensions, you can receive tax relief for contributions up to £40,000 per year.

If you're a basic rate tax payer, you currently get 20% tax relief on your contributions. To save £100 in a personal pensions pot, it only costs you £80. If you're a higher-rate tax payer, you get tax relief on 40% of your contributions, so to save £100 only costs you £60. This easily beats the LISA returns rate of 25% so opt for a personal pension if your earnings are high.

When withdrawing the cash from LISAs and Personal Pensions in retirement, they're treated differently for tax purposes. For a LISA, you've effectively paid the tax on your original contributions already so you when you hit 60 years old, you can withdraw as much of your LISA pot and not pay a penny extra. With a personal pension, you can have a bigger pot overall, but you can only withdraw 25% of your pension pot tax-free. You can access your pension 5 years earlier though from the age of 55. Anything over and above the initial 25% is taxed just like your income was during your working life, so this needs to be taken into consideration when retiring.

Another advantage for a pension is saving into a pension doesn't impact any benefit entitlements. If you're unfortunate enough to need access to benefits at some point in your life and you have a LISA, the amount in your LISA will be taken into account for any means-tested benefits. There's a risk you could be forced to withdraw your money and pay the 25% penalty even though you don't want to.

This is after all, just about pensions. Having every single penny of your wealth locked up until you're retired isn't something that I plan on doing, but a good pension is the foundation to investment portfolios. A pension is just one piece of your bigger investment landscape.

To summarise pensions, if you don't want to worry about getting taxed in retirement, you could save a big chunk of cash in a LISA and enjoy the fact you're not handing any more money over to the government when you retire. If you're a high-rate tax payer, you should be contributing to a pension because you'll be missing out on a lot of free money from the government. It all comes down to you.

Digital Investment Helpers

Artificial intelligence isn't just for sci-fi films. It's now being used to advise you on your finances. One of the newest and in my opinion most useful additions to the investor's toolkit are all of the electronic helpers that you can get to manage your finances. There are broadly three tiers to digital helpers. "Budget planners" help you visualise, categorise and take control of what you're spending and where you're spending it. "Savings chatbots" are a level up and automate saving money on your behalf so you don't have to. Then there's the fully fledged "robo-advisors" that act as your digital money managers and decide what products you should invest in. The recent introduction of Open Banking, which from January 2018 made it a legal right for regulated financial institutions to give you help managing your money if you want it, means there's a lot of choice amongst these digital helpers. I've tried lots of different ones, therefore any mentioned below get my recommendation.

Budget planner Apps

These are the simplest form of digital investment helper but they still have some surprisingly good features. Most of them are also completely free. My favourite is Money Dashboard.

Money Dashboard (www.moneydashboard.com) is a free online personal money management tool. It's available via the website or you can download the app on your smartphone. It brings together your various money-related accounts on a central dashboard. It includes current accounts, credit cards and savings accounts. The visualisation of your data is really useful and you can set up your own custom home screen of graphs on the website to get a really quick visual overview of how your spending is going. Money Dashboard also automatically categorises your spending into different types, so you can filter your expenses to see exactly where your money is going. You can go back several months with this too. A word of warning, it can be quite a shock the first time you do it! One of my first reactions was *"How are we spending that much?!"* but it served its purpose well. It was eye-opening. It's often easy to think you're spending a certain amount of money on something but when you come to sense-check it against the facts, you could be in for a surprise like I was. We were spending far more on random, unnecessary things than I thought. It showed us where we could afford to cut back without really missing out on anything. You can also set up budgets and it'll show you how much under or over your budget you are for things like food, entertainment, clothes etc.

Savings chatbots

These are chatbots that use smart technology to help you save money. They're unique in that they're not really an app, but a digital helper you speak to via social media such as Facebook messenger. It's like having your own personal finance assistance in robot form. You can type in commands to show you a balance on your account, you can command it to save money and withdraw money. All this is done as if you were talking to one of your friends over Facebook messenger, except it's a robot replying instead of a real human.

My favourite savings chatbot is Plum (www.withplum.com). Plum enables you to automatically save money by using a clever algorithm to deduct just the right amount to save based on your normal spending patterns. This means no two amounts saved by Plum are the same. It'll dynamically change what it puts away. Heavy spending month? It'll reduce how much it saves for you. Have a bit more cash than usual? It'll increase the amount slightly to ring-fence it for you.

You can also tweak a setting that controls how adventurous your saving is and set a savings mood from "Shy" to "Ambitious" depending on how adventurous you're feeling. Plum guarantees it won't take you into an overdraft and if by some unfortunate combination of circumstances or unplanned spending spree it puts you into one, they will cover any overdraft fees. You can request a savings update 24/7 and withdraw money at any time which is returned to you within 24 hours. It'll also give you regular updates on your bank balance via Facebook messages. If talking to a robot puts you off, human operators are still on-hand to Facebook chat, email or call too. Also, if you find you have events coming up in life that need a little bit more spending, then you can stop the automatic savings at any time.

One of the best features about Plum and why it's my favourite is that Plum enables you to use your money to invest in 2 different ways. Plum has its own range of funds which you can invest in with themes that are important to you and risk levels you're comfortable with. You can invest in tech funds, emerging markets or even socially conscious companies via an ethical fund. Plum charges a small fee for this.

Plum is also in partnership with P2P lender RateSetter which means you can invest via P2P lending. There are currently no fees associated with this which is great. You can mix and match between straight savings, RateSetter and plum investments however you want. The link between Plum and the combination of hassle-free investing with RateSetter should really appeal to some investors. This is one of the ways we're investing as a family and it works really well. I think it's great that we have our own robot money manager who decides exactly how much you can afford to invest each month.

Robo-advisors

These are perfect for people who are a bit nervous about making investment decisions but don't want to pay for financial advice. Robo-advisors are essentially digital investment managers. For example, if you wanted to invest using a fund supermarket, you need to pick your own investments as remember from earlier in the chapter, these are all "execution-only" services so you're not getting any advice at all. Robo-advisors act as a digital copy of a real-life personal investment advisor. Instead of interviewing you about your personal circumstances like a financial advisor would, a robo-advisors usually starts with a website form that asks you a detailed set of questions related to your investment goals and risk tolerance. Using this information and special computer algorithms, the robo-advisor will then use automated decision-making tools to "recommend" which of its products you should be investing in and build your personalised investment portfolio with no human intervention.

For a lot of new investors, Robo-Advisors might be the perfect solution. You don't have to worry about picking your own investments – that's all taken care of. The disadvantage is there isn't any choice at all – you don't get to pick anything other than your tolerance to risk. To some, this might feel unsettling just paying money for a service with no idea what you're actually buying. You're trusting these Robo-Advisors to make the right decisions for you after all. That being said, you can still monitor your progress and make changes as and when you want, it depends on how comfortable you are with computerised decisions guiding your finances.

Wealthify is one of the most accessible Robo-Advisors as you can start investing from as little as £1. If you were to invest £100 a month, your monthly fee would be about £1. It's also very easy to add more money and you can add regular or one-off deposits. There's also live chat and phone support available. You can check your plans performance whenever you like and change your risk level or withdraw your money at any time. If you feel confident about investing but not confident about picking the right investments, a robo-advisor is seriously worth considering for a part of, or all of your portfolio.

9 INVESTING AS A FAMILY

Y ou're in the process of revolutionising your family's wealth, and that means bringing the whole family on board. That doesn't mean that everyone has to get involved directly, but you should be sharing any major decisions with your partner if you have one and passing on this knowledge to your children. This is an important chapter for me because I don't want you to make this journey on your own. I love investing as a family and hope you will too. The world that we now live in is full of opportunity but there are also a lot of problems to solve, and I want you to equip your whole family with the financial skills to help out with a lot of those problems.

Money of course doesn't solve everything but money can buy one of the most precious things of all, *time*. Being able to spend money on time-saving things because you've set up your investments means more time spent with your family and a better quality of life. I want you to be in a position to not only pursue the things in life you've always wanted to do, but to continue to do this down the generations, as you get your children interested in investing from an early age. As a father I want to encourage my children to explore the world of investing and the powerful effect it can have on their lives as they grow. Whilst financial independence doesn't fix everything, it opens up an entirely new world of possibilities.

Talking to your partner

If you're a single parent – as my mother was – I really respect you for reading this book because you've not got an easy ride, but you're also the sole decision maker in financial matters, which can be an advantage. If you currently have a partner, chances are you and your partner both contribute to the household income. Just over 71% of two-parent families in the UK have both parents working. Despite this, talking about money is traditionally seen as difficult and money issues are one of the main causes of arguments for couples. Are you planning on involving your partner in your investment journey? Even if you've agreed up front that – because you're the one reading this book – you're the one that wants to start investing, the goal of talking to your partner is to agree on the fact that money is important to improving your lifestyle and that you want to work *together* to achieve it. There's power even in a simple, short conversation.

As well as talking about actually starting to invest your money, it's important to talk about the general state of your finances. Whilst I'm not giving relationship advice, the more your general financial expectations and habits are aligned, the better the end result. For example, there might be areas where you're unnecessarily spending that can be put towards reaching your financial goals instead, or you might get an idea to invest that's prompted from a discussion you may have not had with your partner had you not been open about finances.

Keep it light at first

Start by asking for your partner's advice – even if you don't think you need it, and really listen to the response. A simple *"I've been learning a lot about money lately, what are your thoughts on investing instead of just saving?"* Do you get a blank stare or a raised eyebrow? If you do, try another, *"OK, is there anything you think I should change about my spending habits?"* Make it questions about yourself and don't get all accusatory, you're trying to get a feel for their thoughts on finance.

Whatever the answers – whether you agree with them or not - focus on staying calm. The more you hype things, the worse and more tense the situation will be. You're almost trying to make it borderline boring, especially for the first encounter. This is especially useful if you're not used to talking about money at all. It's almost the "foot in the door", at which point, you can then start to expand in later chats. You read earlier in the book all about the different risk tolerances, so it would be a perfect opportunity to ask your partner if they feel the same, or if there's a mismatch somewhere.

What is the reality right now?

Once you've broken the ice – which may or may not take a few initial talks keeping it light to get to this point – it's time to become aware of your financial reality. It might sound obvious to discuss what your money is spent on and where it's going, but I mean more than just the nuts and bolts of what comes in and what goes out. It's about identifying your *attitudes* to money.

Maybe one of you is an extreme saver or an extreme spender. Do you or your partner shudder at the thought of budgeting? Or do you have an itemised spreadsheet with every single outgoing that's updated religiously every single week? Does money tend to trickle out of the bank accounts or does it disappear in great big chunks?

Maybe it's not that extreme, but you probably know how you both co-operate – or don't co-operate – on money matters. The key thing here is that you're *not trying to fix it,* you're just trying to establish what those things are and if they are going to stop you getting in the way of your goals.

You're much more likely to think of something together which one of you wouldn't have individually if you're both involved in the financial discussions. Regardless of attitudes, you need to define what is reality for you both right now.

I'm trying to emphasise doing this as a team because there will definitely be things that one of you has thought of which the other hasn't. It's also much more motivating to have the support of each other. You're sharing the financial burden which makes the load lighter for you both individually.

Set your goals

Now you've established reality, it's time to start looking forwards. In order to have any success with investing, you need to have financial goals. This is the whole point of investing - meeting your financial goals to meet your *life* goals. Not wishy-washy, vague goals like "more money" or "early retirement", but a tangible financial amount with a defined time-frame. You need to attach a value to them because non-specific goals suffer from moving goalpost syndrome. You'll never be able to measure your progress and your finances will suffer over the long run as you keep the foot off the pedal thinking *"oh maybe I'll do that tomorrow"*. Tomorrow becomes next week, next month and then never.

Start to think of specifics and think of these collectively, with your partner and your children. What are you all passionate about? What can't you wait to do, see, own or build? What are your goals over the next 10 years? Where do you absolutely need to be in life and what do you want that would transform the quality of life? Thinking about defining them in real numbers.

Remember, be specific. Start to turn vague goals like *"more money"* into goals like *"at least 20% of my salary as an investment pot in 5 years' time"*. Instead of saying to yourself *"I want to retire early"*, make the target that you want to *"retire at 45 with at least a total retirement pot of £500,000"*. You might want to save for your children's future house deposit or university fees, it doesn't matter as long as it's specific.

This brings me onto my next goal-setting point. The bigger the goal, the better. They need to be outrageous. Borderline unachievable. Mentally anchoring yourself to that ultra-high level instead of setting the bar too low will mean you'll achieve more than if you set it to something you first thought was realistic. Even if you don't end up achieving what you've set out to achieve, you'll end up with significantly more than if your goal was more realistic from the start.

This method might seem counterintuitive and off-putting. It might seem like you're setting yourself up for failure from the very start, why would you want to do that? It'll feel unnatural at first, but the key is to start small and simple. Most advice about anything to do with investing is bland. You're told to try to keep everything logical and essentially pretend to be a robot. Buying anything, investments included, while emotionally charged is never a good thing, but you need to be motivated about something and it's so important to feel *challenged* by something to get really motivated to achieving it.

There's nothing worse than being over-cautious and too calm. Be annoyed that you aren't where you want to be financially yet. Let it bother you that you don't have the life you want for your family yet. Being annoyed stokes the fires of desire. It's a tremendously powerful motivator and it's something that will help you get your finances in check. When you're annoyed about something enough to take action to change your circumstances, you can begin to change your life.

When I first started, I hated the fact that my hard-earned money was earning absolutely nothing sat gathering dust in a bank account each month. I dreamed of a house with a garden for our kids to play in and to grow veg in the corner, but it seemed unachievable at the time. Now we've been here a few years and that mindset gave me a goal and a route to achieve it. I didn't just sit in the corner and give up, I started to take practical steps to be able to live the life I've always wanted to life, and as far as I'm concerned investing is the smartest way to make your money work for you. Get into the mindset. Be bothered about something to put work into sorting it. Don't bow down and accept you won't achieve things. Work out how you can achieve it.

Identify areas for improvement

There's no point changing things for the sake of it. If you've gone through the motions with your partner, you've read this far in the book, and you already do these things, that's great – apply your finances in the best ways you've both discussed and agreed. Some partners won't be interested and have no interest in being involved, but now you've talked about your goals together, you'll have a much clearer idea how both of you need to combine your resources to make them happen or if anything else needs to change.

But chances are there *will* be something one or both of you can improve that won't take much effort, and it'll help you reach your goals quicker than if you'd just carried on. Now's the time to re-read the money-saving tips in

Chapter 6 because you want as much money working for you as you possibly can, irrespective of whether you're doing it as a team or you're going alone.

Sometimes it's not about what you spend or how you spend it, but where you spend it *from*. Consider simplifying the entire process. Do you have multiple bank accounts? A common setup for a lot of couples is having a joint bank account for bills and an individual account for general "stuff", so there are three places that money can be coming out of at any one time. My partner and I share a single, joint bank account, and we find that works for us, however this does appear to be quite a rare circumstance. Others have their own accounts, and then agreements on who pays what within the household based on their income. Whatever your circumstances, consider what works for you and what doesn't work so well and if there is anything you could do differently to improve the situation.

Keep it going

If you're in it together, don't treat this discussion on money as a one-off. The idea is you're growing your *family's* wealth, so schedule in a regular time each month to have a quick chat about finances in general, not just investing. Keeping it regular means making it second nature to talk about finances. You're then in a much better place to make decisions as you go through life. If 6 or 12 months passes whilst only one of you is managing your finances, then it's easy to lose touch with how much your wealth has changed.

Is one of you more comfortable than the other in managing finances? Are you both interested but do you have different ways of thinking about it? Either way, as you make these discussions regular, you begin to share more of your financial journey and you'll hopefully bring your family closer together in the process.

Persuade your kids to invest

"Is this a joke? What possible interest could my daughter/son have in shares?" is probably what you were thinking as you read the title above this paragraph but yes, I'm serious. I absolutely mean to involve your kids with investing and finance. Sometimes it's hard enough getting them to do their homework, let alone think about buying shares of companies, but you have a chance to change the entire course of their lives if you can equip them with powerful financial skills. You can equip them with some of the most life-changing and best money-making skills in the world and who doesn't want to do that for their children?

I want to tell a short story about legendary investor Warren Buffett. If you don't know him, he's an American business giant, investor, speaker and philanthropist. He's considered one of the most successful investors in the world. His company, Berkshire Hathaway, is currently the third largest company in the world, and owns significant shares in many companies that are household names. These include the likes of Coca Cola, Kraft Heinz, American Express, Apple, Mastercard and Visa. Starting early is the main reason Warren is where he is today. His dad was an investor, and so he was naturally exposed to it from childhood. Investing runs through Warren's veins and because of that, he's now worth a colossal $86 billion. With the help of his dad, Warren bought his first stock, a company called Cities Service, way back in 1941 aged 11. He ended up selling this for a small profit of $2 per share, but more importantly, by then the investing bug had bitten him. He ended up turning a small textile manufacturing company into a multinational investing machine and going on to earn billions over his career.

Would he have done this without an early-years influence from his dad? It's hard to say for sure but I doubt it. That's the real power in getting children involved from an early age and you can be doing this same thing to your children too. Every discussion about money is an opportunity for your kids to learn more about it. As you're currently learning about investing, one of the most under-utilised concepts about money is to make it work for *you*.

Involve them in the management of their own money

Our 4-year-old daughter is very aware that money can be exchanged for goods and services. She understands that giving someone money now results in the appearance of "stuff". It's reached the point where she wants something every time we go to the shops, but she'll also accept that this isn't possible due to affordability. Or, we give her a budget – now she'll graciously acknowledge when she can't have something because it's too expensive. We try to make sure we're regularly talking about the importance of money at home and how there isn't an unlimited supply of money to be able to buy everything instantly. It's an important foundation concept to get across before even beginning to think about involving children actively in their financial futures.

We've talked to our daughter about the concept of saving small amounts of money to put towards a big toy or present, to introduce the notion of working towards something over time. Naturally as a 4-year-old, she doesn't stay interested for very long and neither do we expect her to just yet, but recently she surprised Beth and I by deciding that some of her Christmas money was going to be spent on a new toy and some put away for future. Introducing the thought of saving to young children is important because it also introduces the importance of goals. Working towards those goals is something that they'll need to develop and they'll have a head-start doing this from an early age with you helping them.

Financial discipline certainly isn't going to be picked up overnight by any child, but it's setting the foundations that are vital for when they grow up. Many adults don't even have great financial discipline and it's much easier to learn anything at a young age than it is as you get older and are more set in your ways.

Giving children their own pot of money to be responsible for – with your close guidance and control of course! – is another way you can involve them in learning how to be financially responsible. Both of our children have JISAs. Opening a JISA – as discussed in Chapter 8 – is one of the best possible ways to save money for your children's future. With your help, when they're an appropriate age, it'll act as a tool for them to begin to manage their own finances. Remember, this money is *theirs* and what better way to teach them to become financially responsible than helping them to take some responsibility of their own and maybe even increase the odds of getting a good return on their money? Ownership of something is a powerful incentive to look after it and with your guidance your kids can grow up looking forward to the results of their investments as well as the work their money has put in.

One of the very best things that children have on their side is time. The investments made on behalf of your child are some of the safest investments anyone can make simply because of how long they're invested. Holding investments for lots of years means that any short-term volatility in the stock market is "smoothed out" especially with regular contributions taking advantage of pound-cost averaging and compound interest. Remember, any investments for children in a JISA are also protected from withdrawal until they're 18, so big swings in the prices of investments due to a recession, current events like Brexit, or any other political influences are less impactful over the long term. What might be monthly or even yearly changes in price won't matter if you're invested for the right reasons. With any luck, if you've shared your investment knowledge with them, when they turn 18 and have access to their money, they'll know to keep a portion of it invested for later in life too.

Invest in your children's favourite products

In order to fill up your kids JISAs you're going to have to invest in something so why not get them actively involved in picking what goes in them? Kids learn better when it's fun and engaging, and what better way to make an ordinarily dull topic for kids interesting than to involve some of their favourite brands or products and let *them* take ownership of their favourite stuff. It might sound crazy but it makes a lot of sense. Many adult investors focus their money on what they know and love. I hold technology shares because I'm interested in technology and I'll go out of my way to make sure I research it properly. The concept's no different for kids either, they just need your help doing the investment homework.

As a customer and a parent, you have a lot of "insider" knowledge of your kids' favourite things that you probably haven't realised. You'll know their favourite products, films or music inside and out. Not just for themselves though, but also how popular they are amongst their whole peer group. Is it just a fad? Or is it maybe a rising trend that is worth a closer look at the company behind it? How often do their friends talk about it or pester you about it on birthdays? Don't underestimate this type of research. It might just be the way you spot the next big thing and a great investment opportunity. I've included a few examples below.

Take probably the most well-known example, Disney. I'm sure most children out there have a Disney film as one of their all-time favourites. Disney are the world's largest film producer and since 2005, they have bought Pixar, Marvel Entertainments, Lucasfilm and more recently, in July 2018, shareholders approved the acquisition of Rupert Murdoch's film giant 21st Century Fox. Deals like this have always been key to Disney's strategy – suck up as much intellectual property as possible to keep the kids' interested, parents buying products and cash rolling in. The key thing about the Fox purchase is that they also get Fox's global TV network. This extends the reach of their film and media empire to mean even more viewers for Disney's colossal collection of some of the biggest earning films of all time. Examples include the likes of Avatar and Deadpool.

The Fox purchase also sets them up well for the technology of the future. By buying Fox, Disney also gets the controlling stake in Hulu, an American streaming service that rivals Netflix and Amazon Prime. This means that they're now best-placed to take on one of the biggest growth markets in the world. As of October 2018, global streaming had jumped a massive 63%, so Disney are riding that wave as best as they can.

Another well-known example for your older kids (and some adults!) is Fortnite. It's an extremely popular computer game playable across virtually any games platform. References are everywhere, people are making weird dance moves copying the characters in the game and it almost seems to have taken over the gaming world. It follows a unique "freemium" format where the game itself is 100% free on multiple consoles and platforms. It makes users feel like they're getting a premium experience without a premium price tag. The clever bit is termed "up-selling" where they offer in-game rewards but only if gamers buy a "battle pass" for approximately £8. This is how they make a fortune.

The developer of this game is Epic Games. They're not a publicly listed company so you can't buy shares in them directly, but you can buy shares in Chinese tech behemoth Tencent, which owns 40% of Epic Games. Tencent is the world's largest gaming and social media company and one of the most valuable technology companies in the world. Tencent also owns

5% of Activision Blizzard, the makers of the hugely popular Call of Duty franchise which might also interest the readers and their children who are gamers. That 5% of Activision Blizzard is currently worth about $2.5 billion.

Extending beyond just computer games, Tencent is a great way to get exposure to the types of products your kids are interested in. It offers internet services, smartphones, music and social media services, many of these you won't have heard of in the West but that doesn't mean they're not popular over in China. Tencent's social media/mobile payment app WeChat has over 1 billion monthly users. Tencent also benefits from something called the "network effect", where the value of the business grows as users attract other users (their friends) which creates a cycle of growth and strength across its multiple businesses. It's definitely one to watch.

The final example is a way to give your son or daughter shares in Peppa Pig or Ben & Holly's Little Kingdom with Entertainment One which produces both of those kids' TV shows. They're a media company involved in the production of music, films and other TV series. The company's rights library is currently valued at $2 billion and includes about 80,000 hours of film content. Their film and TV distribution deals include other well-known companies such as Universal Pictures, DreamWorks Pictures, Channel 4, National Geographic and many others.

There are many more options out there, the point I'm trying to make is there is major value when you encourage your *kids* to invest in brands they like. You can help them to take responsibility and really learn how investing can change their lives, equipping them with skills for the future. Instead of just spending their money – or should I say *your* money – to own their products, encourage them to own the businesses that make them.

10 INVESTMENT COSTS AND TAXES

Not too long ago, costs to new investors were high and investing required the annoying process of a stockbroker, financial advisor and the willingness to hand over a big chunk of cash as commission to them. In this day-and-age, your computer and even your smartphone lets you save hundreds and thousands in fees by cutting out the middlemen.

While things are now overall much cheaper and accessible, the types of costs you face when investing can be confusing. There are many different types of costs and taxes – not all will apply – and I'll go through the main ones that do. I'll show you some of my favourite cost-effective platforms to invest on and help you minimise your costs as much as possible. I'll also apply these costs to an example portfolio to show you in practical terms how much money you'll spend for a given amount of investments.

It would be impossible to cover every possible cost out there but this section will make you aware of the most common ones that I believe are applicable to most normal investors.

Holding Costs

First things first, to invest in anything, you need an account with a provider. In the same way you have access to your online banking, you need an online account to invest. These types of investment accounts usually carry a small cost to hold your investments, hence the name "holding costs". Popular examples of providers that have holding costs include AJ Bell Youinvest, Charles Stanley Direct or Hargreaves Lansdown. These charges are sometimes referred to as a "custody" charge depending on where you read. Either way it's essentially the same charge being levied.

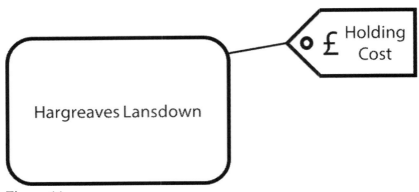

Figure 11

The holding costs are usually a small percentage charged on the total amount of money you invest. For example, my Stocks & Shares ISA held by Hargreaves Lansdown has a holding cost of 0.45% of the value of investment funds and 0.45% of the value of shares, investment trusts, ETFs gilts and bonds. If I had £1000 invested in funds and £500 invested in shares, with the above holding costs, my total holding cost would be:

(0.45% of £1000) + (0.45% of £500) = £4.50 + £2.25 = £6.75 per year

Some account providers charge a fixed cost rather than a percentage. HSBC's InvestDirect service charges you a quarterly account fee of £10.50 and Interactive Investor charges a quarterly fee of £22.50. Big account balances – into the tens of thousands of pounds – often have different levels of charges, so make sure to check with your provider if you're in the position to be investing this much money.

Different account types, even with the same provider, can also have different holding costs. For example, many providers have different charges levied on their non-ISA account and standard share trading account variants. Remember, the main advantage to an ISA is that it protects you from most taxes on your investments, so if you decide to opt for a standard account versus an ISA account variant, make sure you understand the taxes you're liable to pay in future.

Product Costs

This is a separate cost, charged on-top of the account costs for the physical investment you're buying. The most common products that have these are funds. Most funds have what's called an "Ongoing charge", sometimes referred to as an Ongoing Charges Figure (OCF) or a Total Expense Ratio (TER). It's a regular payment that you pay for the management of the fund, usually quoted as an annual charge and expressed as a percentage of the value of the number of units you own of that fund. For example, the HSBC FTSE 250 Index Class S Accumulation fund currently has an OCF of 0.09%. If you had £1000 invested into the fund, the product cost would be £9 per year. Figure 12 shows you how the product cost relates to your investments.

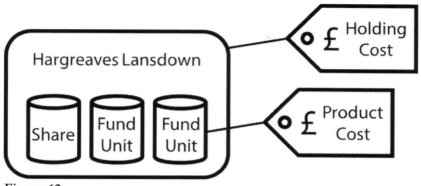

Figure 12

Costs for funds generally vary quite significantly between around 0.09% and 1.5%. Remember back to Chapter 7 and the section on funds, actively managed funds are usually much more expensive because of the constant re-balancing of the fund's portfolio. You're also paying extra for supposed expertise of the fund manager. This additional work managing what's in the fund's portfolio costs more money. Index tracker funds, like the HSBC FTSE 250 Index fund, just follow the proportions of the index they're tracking. As they're effectively a copy of the index, there's no real effort needed to select what goes in them.

Don't underestimate the impact that product costs can have to your overall portfolio. It might not seem like a big difference but over the years it can add up. Table 14 compares the trust HSBC FTSE 250 Index tracker fund against the Hargreaves Lansdown Multi-Manager Special Situations Trust fund.

Amount invested	Fund	Fees per year	Value in 20 years
£1,000 every year	Hargreaves Lansdown Multi-Manager Special Situation Trust	1.50%	£22,084
	HSBC FTSE 250 Index Tracker	0.09%	£25,541
Extra cost due to fees = £3,930			

Table 14

Investing £1000 ever year over 20 years and assuming an equal 3% growth for fairness, the higher fee fund costs you an extra £3,930 in fees. That's nearly 4 years contributions just wiped out. Most people would expect a fund that costs you more money to generate better returns, however as we've also seen earlier in Chapter 7 that isn't true. Just because a product cost is higher, that doesn't guarantee better performance at all. There's a lot of power in tracker funds, as you'll see in the next chapter.

Transaction Costs

Transaction costs are the commissions paid to buy and sell your investments. I've added to the graphic in Figure 13 to represent it graphically. This is another type of cost that varies a lot between different providers and different investment products. For instance, funds usually don't cost much to buy or sell, but shares and ETFs have a big variation in charges depending on who you buy them from.

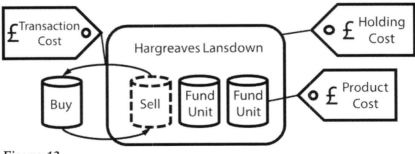

Figure 13

Commissions for the average investor have always been high, with the cost of trading anywhere from around £1.80 to £12.50 per trade for the main stockbrokers, so it's important to shop around. Transaction costs can also be one-off payments or regular. If you want to choose when you buy and sell your investments, you'll usually pay money each time you make a trade.

Many providers also let you set up recurring investments at big discounts to the one-off trading costs. It's a fantastic way to get involved in regular investing. For instance, Hargreaves Lansdown charges £11.95 per deal for individual trades, but if you were to split out your investment over 12 months, you could pay the regular dealing charge of £1.50 – an 87% saving! Barclays' Smart Investor service also offers a discount where you pay a £3 fee per online transaction or £1 for regular investments so make sure you take this into consideration.

Foreign Exchange (FX) costs

Most online stockbrokers make it easy to buy shares from countries outside the UK, but there are usually fees associated with this. Foreign Exchange – referred to as FX – costs are usually payable on all foreign share transactions. This is because many companies don't deal in the foreign currency directly. Your money will be exchanged, then the trade will be made before receiving your shares.

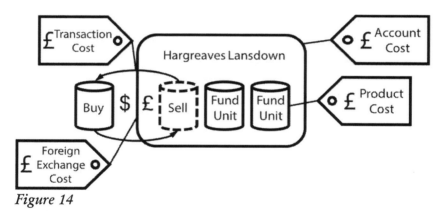

Figure 14

This makes it very convenient to buy and sell foreign shares but you're also left at the mercy of the exchange rate at that particular point in time. This can add extra volatility to the prices of these shares, as not only do you have the company share price fluctuating in value, you also have to deal with the exchange rate doing the same, often completely independently of the company's operations. Depending on your circumstances, I think the choice you have when buying shares from most countries in the world outweighs the extra FX costs.

Miscellaneous Costs

I can't possibly list every different cost from every investment provider in this book, so whilst I've tried to cover all of the main costs, here's a collection of the ones that don't quite fit in any of the boxes above but you still might come across when investing.

Reinvestment Costs

Automatic reinvestment costs are fairly common. If you want any fund income or share dividends automatically reinvested, providers often charge a small percentage of the trade value. If for example you have 1,000 shares that pay a dividend of 10p per share, you'll earn £100 in dividends. Reinvesting the £100 may cost you a certain percentage in fees. Barclays is one provider that doesn't have reinvestment costs for dividends, however AJ Bell Youinvest charges 1%, with a minimum charge of £1.50 and a maximum charge of £9.95.

Telephone dealing costs

Telephone dealing costs are common as there's the added cost of paying someone to take your order over the phone for you. Unless you really like the personal touch when buying things, there's no need to be using any of the provider's telephone services to place orders. Almost all investments you'd want to buy are available to buy via websites and are done automatically.

Paper Statements

Being charged for paper statements is common, as most account providers give you full access to all of your information electronically; but like with most bills these days, if you prefer yours in printed format, you'll have to pay for it.

Account Closure

Account closure costs are usually charged if you transfer out your holdings to a different provider and close an account. This is only if you decide to move your entire holding to a different provider. There's usually some work involved in facilitating the transfer hence the cost. They're usually around £25-£50.

Panel of Takeovers and Mergers (PTM) levy

Something called Panel of Takeovers and Mergers (PTM) levy is a transaction-specific cost and is charged when shares with a total value of over £10,000 are bought or sold. The charge is £1, and goes directly to the PTM. It's an independent body that supervises and regulates company takeovers in the UK.

Popular providers' cost summary

Most investment providers readily display their costs on their websites, but some are much easier to find than others! I've saved you the hassle of having to hunt for them all and summarised the main costs of the most popular providers in Table 15. This isn't an exhaustive list of providers at all but they're the ones I'm most familiar with and have experience using.

Provider	Account Costs	Transaction Costs based on £1000 worth of UK shares in a single transaction	Foreign Exchange Costs
Barclays	0.1% per year (£4 min per month)	£6.00	N/A – Can't trade international shares
Halifax	£12.50 per year	£12.50	1.25%
Hargreaves Lansdown	0.45% of funds + shares	£11.95	1.0%
HSBC	£10.50 per quarter	£10.50	N/A – Varies with each trade.
Interactive Investor	£22.50 per quarter (used towards transaction fees)	£10.00	1.0%
IG.com	£24.00 per quarter	£8.00	0.3%
Degiro	€2.50 per year per exchange traded on outside of LSE	£1.79	0.1%

Table 15

Something to note about Degiro, is that it's great for cheap access to shares, but be aware as they're based in the Netherlands, you can't hold anything bought via Degiro in an ISA, which means paying tax on all of your capital gains. Purely in terms of transaction cost, it's without a doubt the most cost-effective of the main stockbrokers currently available to investors with how cheap it is to trade shares. I've used them for about a year now. Their account was super easy to set up and I can vouch for their customer service as I've asked them several questions and they've always been very quick to reply.

Freetrade is a challenger share trading app that doesn't make the list but gets an honorary mention. At the time of writing they've only just launched and currently have a waiting list for users of their service. They could potentially revolutionise the retail investing landscape by almost completely getting rid of costs for individual investors. Their unique approach means it's completely free to hold and trade shares, but the catch is, the shares are traded at the end of the day, so you don't get a live price. To take advantage of an instant trade means paying. Even though it's early days, Freetrade are definitely one to watch in my opinion, and you can visit their website at www.freetrade.io

To summarise investing costs, they're a necessary evil. Obviously, nothing in this world comes free and that includes making money. You should always look to minimise your costs where you can but you also need to think about a combination of price and service. There are some investment providers like Barclays and Hargreaves Lansdown that offer free investment research updates. I currently have an ISA with Hargreaves Lansdown because I value that additional service as a useful tool when investing. I look at the costs they charge in relation to other providers who are cheaper, but don't offer this service, and for the difference I personally would rather pay for the added analysis you get. Whatever provider(s) you decide to use for investing always read what the full costs are. You might want to ask yourself, *"Will I be using my account provider's investment updates as one of the major sources of my investment research?"* If in doubt, start off investing as cheaply as possible. Pick the provider with the lowest overall charges and go for there. If you find you're getting poor value for money in terms of information, maybe consider switching it up in subsequent years. On the other hand, if you find you're absolutely fine doing all of your own research about your investments, keep costs as low as possible.

Taxes

This section isn't intended to give a detailed overview of what's applicable to your specific circumstances. Everyone's tax situation is highly specific and I couldn't possibly cover it all here, but it will give you a flavour of the types of taxes that are payable when you buy and sell investments as part of your portfolio. Further information on all the taxes listed here, including how to pay them, can be found on the www.gov.uk website.

Stamp Duty

When you buy shares, if you're reading this guide, you'll most likely be doing it electronically. Any UK shares you buy, will be liable for a form of stamp duty tax. The electronic version of stamp duty applicable to UK shares is called Stamp Duty Reserve Tax (SDRT). The tax is taken automatically when you buy your shares electronically so you usually don't need to do anything else. SDRT is charged at 0.5% of the value of the shares. You don't have to pay this tax if you're given shares for free or buy shares from outside the UK. Stamp duty is also only applicable to shares. You're not charged SDRT on funds.

Capital Gains Tax (CGT)

CGT is a tax on the profits– the "gains" – you make when you sell your assets. Capital gains are usually payable on shares, non-government bonds and funds, but it also applies to anything that's considered an investment such as works of art, property, bottles of wine and valuable collectibles.

Each person has an annual capital gains tax allowance (similar to the income tax personal allowance), known officially as the "Annual Exemption Amount". The rate at which the CGT is applied also depends on your total taxable income. The 2018/2019 rates and tax-free allowance figures are show in Table 16.

CGT Annual Exemption Amount	£11,700 for 2018/2019
Standard rate of CGT	10% on investments, 18% on residential property
Higher rate of CGT	20% on investments, 28% on residential property

Table 16

For most people making reasonable gains, and especially for those just starting investing, you probably won't need to worry about this tax for a while, but it's important you know what it is and how to reduce it legally. Here's an example below to paint a clearer picture:

In 2018/2019, let's imagine your total income for the year before tax is £35,000. You've also done spectacularly well with a high-profile tech start up whose share price has just jumped on their latest earnings report. You decide to sell £20,000 worth of your shares. These only cost you £5,000 to buy. Your capital gain is therefore £15,000, which is the amount you're liable to pay tax on.

Your taxable income is your income before tax (£35,000) minus the personal tax allowance (£11,850). This affects how much CGT you pay on this sale. This leaves you with your taxable income as per Table 17.

Income before Tax	£35,000
Personal Tax allowance for 2018/2019	£11,850
Taxable Income	£35,000 - £11,850 = £23,150

Table 17

You also need to know what the upper limit of the basic rate tax band is. This is the basic rate tax limit (£46,350 for 2018/2019) minus the personal tax allowance. The upper limit is shown in Table 18:

Basic Rate Tax limit for 2018/2019	£46,350
Personal Tax allowance for 2018/2019	£11,850
Upper limit of the basic rate band	£46,350 - £11,850 = £34,500

Table 18

If your total taxable income (£23,150) plus the gains on your shares (£15,000) minus the CGT annual exemption (£11,700) are less than the upper limit of the basic rate income tax band (£34,500), the rate of CGT on your investments is 10% as shown in Table 19. For any gains or any part of gains above that limit, this pushes you into the higher rate tax band so the CGT rate would be 20% for your investments.

Taxable Income	£23,150
Capital Gains on shares	£15,000
Taxable Gains on shares	£15,000 - £11,700 = £3,300
Taxable Income + Taxable Gains	£23,150 + £3,300 = £26,450

Table 19

As your taxable income plus your taxable gains is less than the upper limit of the basic rate band, the CGT rate on your sale would be 10%. Your CGT annual exemption allowance luckily eats up most of the gains you've made, leaving only £3,300 to pay tax on. Therefore, your final CGT bill is £330 for profiting £15,000.

The most important point about CGT is that you don't pay a penny in tax when you sell most investments that are held in an ISA, which is why as I've said previously it's so important to make sure you're using as much of your ISA allowance as possible each year.

One of the best things about CGT allowances is that if you're married, you and your partner can effectively combine your individual allowances together. In order to reduce the tax that you pay, a married couple or civil partnership can get up to £23,400 tax-free capital gains this tax year. You can transfer investments between your spouse/civil partner tax-free, so it might make sense to consider transferring holdings to a spouse in a lower tax bracket or one who hasn't used their allowance.

Dividend Tax

Shares that you own might be paying out dividends each year. If they do, you only have to pay dividend tax if you go above your dividend allowance in the tax year. For the 2018/2019 tax year, the annual dividend allowance is £2,000. This is big considering that most dividends are paid in pence per share, so you'd have to own a lot of shares in dividend-paying companies to break this limit. For the average investor, it's unlikely to be something to worry about. If you do have a large number of shares, you'll have to take this into consideration.

Interest Tax

Basic rate tax payers get £1,000 of tax-free savings each year. Your allowance applies to any interest from money in bank accounts (which sadly probably isn't very much), any funds paying income classed as interest, any P2P lending and interest from bonds. If you go over this allowance, your usual rate of income tax is applied, which once again shows why an ISA is so important as any UK investments held in an ISA are free from these taxes.

Withholding Tax

You might have to pay tax if you have foreign shares and those companies pay out dividends. This tax is known as a "withholding tax" and the rate varies between 15% and 35% depending on the country. You can usually claim this money back, however the UK has negotiated a double taxation agreement with some countries, meaning you're exempt from paying the additional tax.

This is important as this impacts any foreign shares held in an ISA. Despite ISAs and their normal tax-free status, withholding tax is one of the rare examples of having to pay tax on earnings sheltered inside an ISA. It's because you're not paying tax to the UK government in this case, which doesn't fall under the usual tax-free banner of everything else in an ISA.

Inheritance Tax

Inheritance tax can be payable in certain circumstances. It's even liable on ISA pots. ISAs are considered part of your estate for inheritance tax purposes. The current lifetime asset limit for inheritance tax is £325,000 before any inheritance tax is due, but anything above that will be taxed at

40%.

Example costs on a portfolio

When I started investing, I struggled really hard to find practical examples that gave me all the information I needed to know about the cost of investing. It took a lot of trial and error and research, switching between different books and websites before I built up a full picture of costs I needed to pay. Now that you know about each of the main investing costs, let's take it one step further to see how they combine in a portfolio. The first time I did this exercise with my own portfolio several years ago, it all clicked together and I hope you won't have to go through that same pain of being caught off-guard by costs. Just a small note, investing costs are fairly standard whatever your circumstances, however your taxes are specific to you as an individual so it wouldn't have been useful to include taxes (other than stamp duty) in this example, therefore the example below focuses on costs only.

For simplicity, I've not assumed any growth to investments in the example as this makes it easier to show costs. I've also not included any of the miscellaneous costs described in the costs section as these aren't typical for most new investors.

A bit about Tim

Let's use our imaginary friend Tim for this example. He's decided to start investing his money. He's sick and tired of the ultra-low interest rates in savings accounts and wants to change his family's way of life. Tim's used all the tips in this book plus some other savings to a total of £10,000 to invest. Tim's new to investing, 30 years old, has a wife and has a daughter. He isn't bothered by short term volatility, because there's a lot of time for his investments to ride it out and hopefully gain in value. This means he has quite a high tolerance to risk. He wants to split his money between funds and individual shares, ignoring any bonds/property for the time being as he thinks these give better overall risk-to-reward for the long term for his circumstances.

Tim decides to make an up-front investment of £3,000 into a fund. He then decides that every month, he'll contribute £300 to the same fund to take advantage of pound-cost averaging, so in total he spends £3,000 + (£300 x 12) = £6,600 in a year on funds. He'd also like some exposure to some individual companies as he's been reading about some up-and-coming potential investment opportunities, so he decides to invest the remaining £3,400 of his money in UK shares. He spaces this out equally through the year, buying about £567 worth of shares every other month. His portfolio is represented in graph form in Figure 15. Tim's decided to do all of this with Barclays as he's familiar with the bank and thinks the charges are fairly reasonable.

The cost breakdown

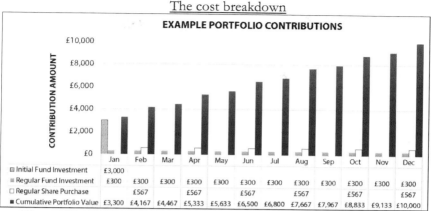

EXAMPLE PORTFOLIO CONTRIBUTIONS

	Jan	Feb	Mar	Apr	May	Jun	Jul	Aug	Sep	Oct	Nov	Dec
Initial Fund Investment	£3,000											
Regular Fund Investment	£300	£300	£300	£300	£300	£300	£300	£300	£300	£300	£300	£300
Regular Share Purchase		£567		£567		£567		£567		£567		£567
Cumulative Portfolio Value	£3,300	£4,167	£4,467	£5,333	£5,633	£6,500	£6,800	£7,667	£7,967	£8,833	£9,133	£10,000

Figure 15

Tim's holding costs are based on the annual contributions to his portfolio and they're split between funds and shares. Based on Barclay's costs, 0.2% is charged on the initial £3,000 investment plus each month's regular £300 fund investment he makes, totalling £6,600 for the year. 0.1% is charged on the 6 share purchases of £567 per year, totalling just over £3,400. Table 20 shows that because the total fund and share charges are below Barclay's £48.00 threshold, that's the minimum charge for his holdings.

	Funds	**Shares**
Holdings Costs	0.2% of £6,600 (total yearly fund investment)	0.1% of £3,402 (total yearly share investment
	£13.20	£3.40
	Sub-Total	
	Funds and share costs combined are less than the minimum of £48.00, so Tim's charge = £48.00.	

Table 20

There are a few transaction costs to pay as Tim invests several times throughout the year. These are shown in Table 21. The lump sum payment of £3,000 he spends on funds in January costs him £3. The other 6 lots of shares every other month cost £6 per purchase. His £300-a-month he spends on buying funds costs him £1 per month. Stamp duty is payable on shares, which is a standard 0.5% of his annual spend on shares. All of these transaction costs add up to £68.00.

		Funds	**Shares**
Transaction Costs	**Dealing Charges**	£3 per one-off fund purchases (£3 x 1 lump sum of funds)	£6.00 per share purchase (£6 x 6 lots of shares)
		£3.00	£36.00
	Regular Investment Fees	£1 per month for monthly fund purchases	N/A as no monthly share purchases
		£12.00	£0.00
	Stamp Duty	Stamp Duty isn't applicable to funds	0.5% of £3,400 (total yearly share investment)
		£0.00	£17.00
		Sub-Total	
		Dealing Charges + Regular Investment Fees + Stamp Duty = £68.00	

Table 21

Tim decided to buy the iShares Emerging Markets Equity Index fund as shown in Table 22. This is the only product cost he pays as he doesn't get charged any product costs for buying any shares. He's only bought the one fund in this example, so the fund's OCF – the charge paid to the manager of the fund – is 0.23% at the time of writing. As he's invested £6,600 into it over the year, his total product costs for the year are 0.23% of £6,600 = £15.18.

Product Costs	**Fund Name**	iShares Emerging Markets Equity Index Fund
	Ongoing Charge	0.23% of £6,600 (total yearly fund investment)
	Sub-Total	£15.18

Table 22

Adding all of the numbers up, the total charges for the year for Tim's portfolio are:

Holding Costs (£48.00) + Transaction Costs
(£68.00) + Product Costs (£15.18) = £131.18

Tim's portfolio of size of £10,000 means this represents about 1.3% of the total amount that Tim has invested. Remember, this is excluding any growth in your investments for simplicity, but you now hopefully have a feel for the level of cost you should be paying for a given amount of money.

When you invest, you don't have to work out any of these costs manually by the way. They're all entirely automatic with any provider, but I hope this demystifies these charges when you can see them worked out in front of you. You can substitute any numbers you want into the example above to make it reflect your own personal circumstances depending on what you want to do, and use the rough guide of 1.3% of your investment amount to get an idea of what it might cost you.

11 JUST FOUR SIMPLE STEPS

Enough with the theory, now it's time for some action. You've read enough to be able to start your investment journey. I want to introduce the four simple steps to making your first investment. One of the main goals when I set out writing this book was to get rid of the barriers many people had to investing and as with most things, getting started is often the hardest part. It's overwhelming how many different options there are out there and paralysis analysis is a real thing in this day and age, so this section should give you some real, actionable suggestions.

Step #1 – Analyse your current financial situation

Are you where you want to be financially? Chances are no, not many people are. It's also why you're reading this book. First, work back through all of the content in Chapter 6. Check that you've set up your budget, free up as much cash as you can and how much you can afford to invest each month with your newly saved money. That's the most important bit. This *needs* to be affordable. Investing any money that isn't sustainable just won't work. By working out what you can regularly afford, you'll build in consistency and discipline.

Once you've done that, revisit Chapter 9 and talk to your partner about goals. Hopefully you've already done it at this point but either way, sit down together and work out your long-term and short-term goals. This is *why* you're investing in the first place. Do you want a new house, a new car, to be financially free, an early retirement? Is there something you just can't stop thinking about day and night? Whatever it is, fixate on it and commit to achieving it. Remember, this is why you're making all these changes and investing in your future.

Step #2 – Open a Stocks and shares ISA account

Now you have your money and your goals. Next is setting up an account ready to buy your investments. In simple terms, you have two main options when it comes to how you want to proceed. All the different types of investments listed in this book can be bought using a computer, mobile phone and internet connection. Don't be afraid to shop around either. You do the same for shopping for the best deals on electronics, the same applies to investments!

Option 1

Open an ISA with a low-cost, reputable, online provider. Pick one of the fund supermarket providers discussed in Chapter 10. Don't bother with your high-street bank. It's too restrictive as you won't have the choice that you have with an online provider. Do you prefer the lower-cost, no-frills providers? Are you happy to pay a slightly higher fee in exchange for more information? Even if you're not 100% sure, pick one and commit for now. It doesn't have to be perfect; you can swap your ISA provider at any point with minimal hassle. The main thing you need is that tax-free wrapper for all of your hard-earned cash.

Option 2

If you're not quite prepared to pick your own investments, select a good Robo-Advisor like Wealthify as discussed in Chapter 8 and create an account. Make sure it's an ISA account as many robo-advisors offer both normal and ISA account variants. Remember, an ISA is necessary to protect your gains from tax, so if you can take advantage of it you definitely should be. On your chosen Robo-Advisor's website, answer all the necessary questions so that you can get some suggestions on where to invest your money to match your investment risk appetite.

Step #3 – Set up a direct debit

Once your account is open, set up a direct debit. This can start from as little as £1 a month depending on which provider you pick. You want to automate the investment process as much as possible. The way I like to look at it, is that you've psychologically committed to put that bit of money to work. It's more difficult to spend the money on other things if you've automated the process.

If you're setting up a direct debit with an online account provider like the ones listed back in Chapter 10 your regular contributions can work in one of two ways. Either you can regularly deposit cash into your ISA for investing later, or you can select your chosen investments and buy them automatically each month. You'll then buy the maximum number of units for the money you want to spend. For example, if you wanted to buy shares of fast food company Just Eat, their current share price is 696p. If you had £100 a month to invest and only bought these shares, you'd get approximately 14 shares (excluding any fees).

If you're not sure about exactly what investments you want to spend your money on, just stick to cash for now. You don't need to choose your investments straight away. Once the cash is in your ISA allowance for the year, then it's in that all-important tax-free wrapper for as long as you want.

Remember from Chapter 7, regular investments allow you to take advantage of pound-cost averaging and they also fit in great with being part of your monthly pay packet from work. This time, instead of an extra bill, this money is being put to work for your future, your kid's future inheritance, a new house, a new car, an early retirement, whatever you want.

Step #4 – Pick your investment!

Depending on how comfortable you are with picking your own investments – and you should at least be more comfortable now than before reading this book – you should either use a Robo-Advisor as discussed or select a good quality fund. I've given you some suggestions below based on what I think are good investments.

Before pulling the trigger and paying for any investment, remember, the value of your money can go down as well as up, there are no guarantees with investing. Make sure you consider your risk tolerance as discussed in Chapter 5. You need to be investing in products that match your level of risk. Don't force this and think you need to take bigger risks than you're comfortable with or you're going to self-sabotage and scare yourself away from the very start. Funds have a risk level that's shown on their key information documents when you do a search on the internet.

My fund top picks

Funds – particularly index tracker funds – are the easiest investments to start with but also the most sensible, as they have maximum spread of investments, minimum effort and minimum cost. Individual shares can make up a good part of the ideal portfolio, but not so much for new investors. It forces you to put all your eggs in one basket, and depending on your choice, which could be inexperienced, the one or two individual shares could perform very badly which could knock your confidence.

You can still get it wrong with funds but it's easier to get it right too. You should absolutely focus on funds first and foremost, then everything else follows as you gain confidence and skills. Here's a list of three current funds I think are great starting points to give you some ideas. These are my own opinions, based on my personal risk tolerance. They might not be suitable for you, but they should hopefully make you think. All three of these funds, when combined, offer global exposure in the UK, emerging markets and the developed world. They're also some of the lowest cost products out there.

HSBC FTSE 250 Index Tracker Fund

The main aim of this fund is to provide long-term capital growth by matching the return of the FTSE 250. The FTSE 250 is a mid-cap index which is made up of the 250 largest companies outside of the largest 100, which are represented by the FTSE 100. This fund is a full replication tracker fund; therefore, it aims to invest in all of the companies that make up that index in the same proportions as the index itself. This fund has an on-going charge of 0.09% which is one of the lowest charges out there. The total investment growth over the last 5 years for this fund is 31.3% which is good.

I think this is a great fund to invest in because it takes advantage of the "mid-cap sweet spot" as discussed in Chapter 7. It's also comprised of only UK companies, so it's great if you wanted to invest domestically rather than internationally. That means no FX costs to pay. However, it is also at the mercy of events within the UK economy and has heavy weighting toward the financial services sector. As new challenger banks come along to disrupt the UK financial services market, there could be an interesting future for this fund.

iShares Emerging Markets Equity Index Fund

This fund's aim is to provide long-term capital growth by tracking the performance of the FTSE Emerging Index. The fund invests in the shares of companies that make up the emerging markets index which includes Asia, African and the Middle East. As such, most of the shares owned by this fund are from companies based there.

Emerging markets are generally more sensitive to economic and political issues than developed markets so expect high volatility and high risk but there are potentially big gains to be made too. International markets are also sensitive to changes in currency which could also affect the value of your investments. This fund has an on-going charge of 0.23%. The total investment growth over the last 5 years for this fund is a very good 43%.

Investments in emerging markets have the potential to grow massively in the future and it's where I've focused a large part of my own investment portfolio. As of 2018, according to the International Monetary Fund, global gross domestic product (GDP) which is the total value of goods and services produced during one year across the whole world, was split 40% advanced economies to 60% emerging markets. Emerging markets are a really important player in the future of the world. This gap is predicted to widen even more as the years go on and with emerging markets accounting for so much global production, this is good news for companies in those industries.

Vanguard FTSE Dev World ex UK Equity Index Fund

This fund's aim is to provide long-term capital growth by tracking the performance of the FTSE Developed Index – excluding the UK. This means the fund is made large and mid-cap international companies including those from North America, Japan, France, Switzerland and Canada. It's a great pick for UK-based investors looking for international exposure that aren't comfortable with investing in emerging markets due to their risk tolerance. This fund has an on-going charge of 0.15%. The investment growth over the last 5 years for this fund is a fantastic 74%, largely driven by the growth in the technology shares this fund holds.

By owning this fund you'll be owning some very notable brands such as Apple, Microsoft, Amazon, Facebook and Alphabet – the parent company of Google. This gives you good exposure to the technology sector which has been historically under-represented in UK companies. As this fund also doesn't have any UK exposure, it avoids any potential UK political issues.

DARIO CHIN

12 ADVANCED CONCEPTS

The simple four-step method in the previous section will get you started just fine, but in case your thirst for knowledge hasn't yet been satisfied, here's some information about more advanced investing concepts. You'll hopefully be able to use some of these techniques to help you as your journey progresses so you'll know what you're looking for and how to go about maximising the odds of good returns on your portfolio.

Asset allocation and diversification

Simplistically speaking, asset allocation is what assets you decide to keep in your portfolio and diversification is how different those assets are to one another. To the new investor, asset allocation and diversification can be easily achieved by the 4-step method outlined in the previous chapter. A fund is a natural example of asset allocation in practice as you'll see as you read on, however as you move along your journey, you'll need to understand these concepts in greater detail when you want to start picking individual investments and growing your portfolio. This can then be used to keep you on track to your goals.

Strategic Asset Allocation

The process where you decide how much of your money you are willing to allocate to particular types of assets is called – unsurprisingly – asset allocation. Owning just a single asset class is very risky, because wild swings in the market can mean wild swings in value of your entire portfolio. For example, if you invested all your money in UK Commercial Property in 2014, you would have made around a 19.5% return that year. In 2016 though, that return would have only been around 2.6%.

There are multiple types of asset allocation available for investors to use, but one of the most effective and useful is called "Strategic Asset Allocation". The concept is fairly simple. You assign a fixed percentage of your portfolio to an asset and keep it that way. As a reminder, the four main asset classes are shares, bonds, cash and property, so I'll use them in an example. Let's assume you decide that after 18 months investing in a single fund, you want to broaden your exposure to the different asset classes so you decide to set up your portfolio to comprise 75% as shares, 10% as bonds, 5% as cash and 10% as property. Figure 16 shows this graphically.

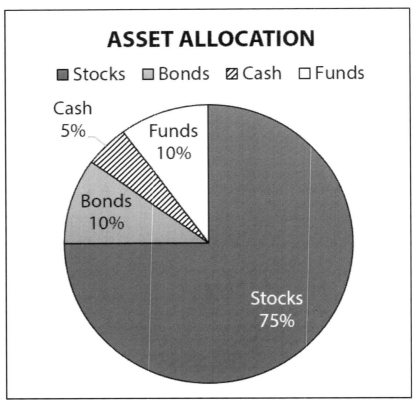

Figure 16

The way that strategic asset allocation works is that you review the proportions of your investments based on their performance and re-balance your portfolio at regular, pre-defined intervals. Once a year is a good interval, shorter or longer can work but you shouldn't really be looking to do this more than once every six months as this will result in too much trading taking place, with insufficient time for your investments to actually "do" anything in terms of growth. Strategic asset allocation is a minimum-trade strategy. You should be making as few investment trades as necessary to get your portfolio mix right as otherwise, you'll pay a lot in fees which will eat into your returns. Set it, forget it (for a period), review it, change it, then repeat.

As an example, suppose it's 2017, you have just inherited a £20,000 lump sum, and you decide the strategic asset allocation as per Figure 16 is appropriate for your tolerance to risk.

Asset Class	Target Allocation	Starting amount in 2017
Shares	75%	£15,000.00
Bonds	10%	£2,000.00
Cash	5%	£1,000.00
Property	10%	£2,000.00
Target Allocation	100%	£20,000.00

Table 23

Let's also assume that over the last year, your shares have grown 8%, bonds have earned 3%, cash has earned 0.5% and property has grown 6%. For simplicity in this example, we will assume all bond earnings are re-invested – compounded – to buy more bonds.

The current value of your portfolio is as per the righthand column in Table 24. Each of your assets have increased in value at different rates, which has resulted in the overall percentage allocation of each asset class in your portfolio changing. Table 24 shows how the percentage has changed compared to what it was in Table 23. For shares, your £15,000's worth has grown 8% so are now worth £16,200. This is now 75.75% of the new total portfolio rather than your original target allocation of 75%. The other 3 asset classes however have decreased and are all less than your initial target percentages. The whole point of strategic asset allocation is that you maintain the same allocation of assets in your overall portfolio so therefore you need to make some adjustments.

Asset Class	2018 Allocation	Amount in 2018	Interest Rate
Shares	75.75%	£16,200.00	8.0%
Bonds	9.63%	£2,060.00	3.0%
Cash	4.70%	£1,005.00	0.5%
Property	9.91%	£2,120.00	6.0%
Target Allocation	100.00%	£21,385.00	–

Table 24

To keep your asset allocation the same as when your portfolio was set up, you need to sell some of your shares and use more money for cash, buying bonds and property. As per Table 25, you would sell £161.25 worth of shares, and split the proceeds across bonds/cash/property. You're now back to your target allocation percentages. This is referred to as "re-balancing".

Asset Class	Target Allocation Percentage	Target amount (A)	Amount in 2018 (B)	Adjustments needed (A-B) for correct target allocation
Shares	75%	£16,038.75	£16,200.00	-£161.25
Bonds	10%	£2,138.50	£2,060.00	£78.50
Cash	5%	£1,069.25	£1,005.00	£64.25
Property	10%	£2,138.50	£2,120.00	£18.50
Target Allocation	100%	£21,385.00		

Table 25

Not re-balancing doesn't mean that everything will be a disaster, but it does mean your portfolio risk is changing over time based on how your investments perform. You could simply just leave the relevant percentages as they were each year, and that might be OK, but after a while, if you're just accepting any percentage of any asset in your portfolio, you're essentially changing the overall risk of your portfolio from what you originally decided when you wanted to start investing. That's why this concept is so important. It takes emotions out of the equation and means you're consistent with your investing decisions over the long term. Better clarity means better chance of maximising yours and your family's wealth.

I recognise that when you start investing it'll be difficult to fit all of the recommended asset types into your portfolio from the start, which is why picking a fund is a good choice as in most cases this automatically allocates your investment based on the fund's goals. I definitely didn't have enough money or time at the very start of my investing journey to make a nice balanced-risk portfolio, but you don't need big sums of money to do this and you don't need to do this all in one go. Just start with what you have. The aim over time will be to add different assets to the mix so that you've eventually got a variety of assets in your portfolio.

<u>Diversification</u>
Diversification is effectively the next "level" up from asset allocation.

It's one of the most important but misunderstood aspects of investing. You've spread your money over the asset classes with asset allocation, now you're looking *within* each class to diversify each class of assets. It's making sure that within each asset class, there's enough variety so you have a broad mix of assets from all types of different industries, geographical regions and sizes.

Many investors make the mistake of thinking that by picking their different asset classes – with asset allocation – that this automatically creates a well-diversified portfolio but this is wrong. You could perfectly allocate your portfolio's assets but be very poorly diversified. The most obvious example is if you were to make your portfolio entirely out of assets from the same country. The diversification here is non-existent as every asset in your portfolio is then subjected to any economic or political risks from that country, which could cause issues.

It's important to understand though, that diversification isn't done to maximise performance, it's done to get the best balance between return and risk. A factor that's important to diversification is something called "correlation".

Different types of asset classes are affected in different ways by things such as interest rates, politics, conflicts, even weather. What's positive for one can be negative for another. Think of an umbrella company and an ice cream company. If you invested in both companies your returns on the umbrella company would be good during rainy months, but the ice cream company's returns are poor when it's raining. The reverse happens when the weather is sunny. This is an example of perfect negative correlation. One is going up as the other is going down. As you sell more ice cream when its sunny, the ice cream cone manufacturer sales also increase. This is an example of perfect positive correlation. Their sales move in the same direction.

Ideally you want to invest in companies that are as least correlated as physically possible, which means there's no relation – either positive or negative – to each other. Why? Because factors affecting one of your assets won't be affecting the other four. If you had five investments, you'd pocket the average return of all five. Assuming they're not correlated, you'd get *less* than the average risk, therefore every "level" of risk you take, you get a better return. It's virtually impossible to find perfectly uncorrelated companies for your portfolio however it's something you need to be aware of to make sure you don't pick things from the same or opposing industries.

There are different ways to diversify and there's no one-size-fits all approach. One example is to diversify by different types of sector as per Figure 17. You've used asset allocation to give you a portfolio that is 75% shares and then that 75% of your portfolio is diversified by making sure the shares are made up of companies from different sectors and industries. In this case it's an even 15% per sector. You could also diversify by region, so for instance, US shares, European shares, Asian or Australian. It could even be a combination of the two. Whilst my example shows how shares can be diversified, it's not just limited to shares. Bonds and property can and should also be diversified. There are lots of ways to achieve a diversified portfolio.

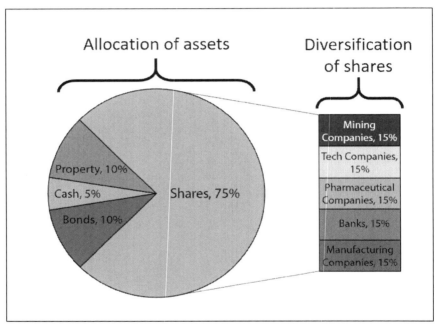

Figure 17

Diversification is useful for exposure to investments that aren't necessarily based in your home country. If you're just starting out investing, you might be looking at shares close to home in the UK in something that's called "home bias". This is where you preferentially pick investments in your own country for no other reason that they're *from* your own country. Whilst you may understand the product or business better for a domestic company, you can fall in to the trap of playing it too safe with domestic investments.

There may be companies and brands you're familiar with, which is a fine place to start when investing, but diversifying forces you to look at other opportunities around the world that you might be missing. Different geographical regions are less likely to be affected by the same types of issues, and therefore be less correlated. A properly diversified portfolio is a very powerful start to your future.

What influences investment prices?

Investment prices can be affected by a wide variety of issues and one of these is the performance of the company. Publicly listed companies usually publish their financial results to investors twice a year. One of these is the "interim" results and the other the "full year" results. They also provide trading updates twice a year too. These figures and statements give the investment community an insight into how a company is performing financially such as how much profit it has earned or planning to earn.

Companies are also required to notify the public about any event that could influence their share price, such as a takeover bid or the launch of a new product. These are known as regulatory announcements and they must be made via a regulatory channel known as an approved RIS (Regulatory Information Service) before the information is published anywhere else. Investors can also find out information on a company from other sources such as newspaper articles, stockbroker reports and specialist websites.

If a company is performing well, and this is expected to continue, the share price of that company should increase. Share prices work on "speculation" which is the general opinion of how a company will perform in the future, not just the present-day situation. This is why you can often see drops in share price even on the face of apparently really good news. Amazon recently reported record-breaking 2018 sales and actually beat the estimates of analysts, bringing over $3 billion in profit. They also announced that they anticipated slower growth in 2019 and weaker profits, so despite the hefty profits now, the share price dropped about 5% lower because of their future forecast. Share prices can be very sensitive to news.

The bulls and the bears

Another major influencing factor for investment prices has a lot to do with bulls and bears. The investment world is full of funny terms. A "bull market" is the term given when everything in the economy is going well, which normally means low levels of unemployment, lower levels of customer borrowing and increase in business output. Investing during a bull market is arguably easier because everything is going up, including people's optimism. If a person is optimistic and believes that shares will increase in price, they're called a bull and are said to have a "bullish" outlook. Bull markets can't last forever though and sometimes they can create dangerous situations if shares become overvalued.

One severe form of a bull market is known as a bubble, where the upward trajectory of stock prices doesn't have any relationship to actual business performance and people's optimism gets completely out of hand. Everyone in an investment bubble is blown away by the amazing prospect of making so much money so fast and it snowballs out of control quickly.

The two major bubbles you're most likely aware of include the "dotcom" technology bubble in the year 2000 and the housing bubble of 2008 that sparked the Great Recession. Bubbles always pop when reality catches up with the sky-high prices. It's only looking back in hindsight that people notice it was actually a bubble. It's difficult to recognise when investors are in a bubble and even harder to predict when it'll pop. There's a lot of thought that cryptocurrency could be the next bubble because of the crazy Bitcoin prices, reaching almost as high as $20,000 per coin at the end of 2017. Time will tell on that one.

A bear market is informally defined as a 20% drop in market indexes. Bear markets happen when the economy appears to be in or near recession which includes rising unemployment and falling business profits. A strategy that a lot of people follow, but that I don't recommend, is to wait on the side-lines until you feel that the bear market is nearing its end, but when you try to "time" the market like this, you'll never be able to predict for sure when things are about to change. Read more about this in the Hints and Tips chapter next.

Bear markets are typically associated with an increase in stock market volatility, since as we previously discussed, at an emotional level investors fear loss more than they feel good about gains. People aren't rational actors – especially when it comes to money and investments. When markets are faced with millions of irrational people, markets in general don't behave rationally. Prices don't rise or drop in an orderly or rational way but rather market participants often overreact in panic and can send prices swinging wildly. More on panic and investing – and what to do about it – in the next chapter.

Famous investing numbers

There are hundreds of different techniques available for assessing the value of companies but only a handful are both practical and useful. Using more techniques doesn't mean you'll end up with a better decision. If anything, it'll work the opposite way and it's easier to second-guess yourself by adding in complexity to your decision-making, rather than just sticking to a few basic, tried-and-tested methods that are used across the industry. All of these numbers for most major businesses are readily displayed on multiple websites.

Price-to-Earnings Ratio (P/E Ratio)

This is one of the most popular ways of valuing a stock. I'm not including it for its popularity though; it's generally one of the simplest concepts to check and it's very useful too. The P/E ratio measures a company's current share price in relation to how much money it earns per share of issued stock. It's the share price divided by earnings per share. An example is the following: Widget Enterprises is trading at £20, and the earnings-per-share (sometimes called EPS) for the most recent 12-month period is £4, then Widget Enterprises has a P/E ratio of 20/4 = 5. If you were to buy shares of this company, you're investing £5 for every £1 of earnings.

Generally speaking, the lower the P/E ratio the better. The ratio can also be thought of as the number of years it will take the company to earn back the amount of your initial investment assuming that earnings stay constant. For example, if you really love their widgets and you see great prospects for the widget business, you might decide to buy 100 shares of Widget Enterprises for £2,000. Current earnings-per-share are £4, so your 100 shares will "earn" £400 the next coming year. Your original outlay of £2,000 will be earned back in 5 years if things stay constant. The P/E ratio removes having to do this calculation for each and acts as a form of shorthand.

P/E ratios aren't any use on their own, they need to be compared with other P/E ratios in the same industry. Comparing across industries won't give you meaningful results because different industries will have different ranges. For example, software companies might sell at an average P/E ratio of 20, but clothing manufacturers might only trade at a P/E of 8. It doesn't mean that all clothing manufacturers are better buys than software companies because of their lower P/E ratios, it just means you're trying to compare apples to oranges.

Within industries the P/E ratio serves as a useful tool to evaluate a shares performance. For example, if you had a choice between Widget Enterprises and you knew their P/E ratio was 5, or Gizmo Industries and you knew their P/E ratio was 2.5, all else being equal, you should choose to buy Gizmo Industries shares. This is because you're getting double the earnings power and the shares are "cheaper" on a relative basis.

Debt-to-Equity Ratio (D/E Ratio)

When a lot of people read "debt" they usually think of something that should be avoided – credit cards/loans/bills all come to mind, but when you're running a business debt isn't all bad. In fact, a lot of investors want companies to use debt in a smart way to fund business projects and ultimately growth, as this all adds up to returns to you as a shareholder. Investors will rarely want to buy shares of a company with a really low debt-to-equity ratio because this shows that the company isn't using *any* debt to finance expansion projects or operations which will limit the total returns for you. Some debt is good, a lot of debt is bad and this is essentially what the D/E ratio tells you.

D/E ratio shows how much debt a company is using to finance its activities when compared to the value of the company's shares. This is how leveraged a company is. The debt acts as a "lever" that makes it easier to fund those expansion projects and other activities.

It's shown on the company balance sheet and should be readily searchable on the internet so you don't have to work this out yourself but it's useful to understand how to. D/E ratio is calculated by dividing a company's total debt by shareholders' equity:

$$D/E\ Ratio = Total\ Liabilities\ /\ Shareholders'\ Equity$$

Essentially, we're trying to find out how much does the company own versus how much does the company *owe*. It's the same sort of thing that a bank would want to know if you were taking out a loan or a mortgage.

Let's look at an example. Here's the balance sheet of Widget Enterprises in Table 26:

Widget Enterprises Balance Sheet	
Short-Term Debt	£4,000,000
Long-Term Debt	£12,000,000
Total Debt	**£16,000,000**
Common Shares	£500,000
Preferred Shares	£250,000
Additional Paid in Capital	£6,000,000
Retained Earnings	£3,000,000
Total Shareholder's Equity	**£9,750,000**

Table 26

Using the debt-to-equity formula, the debt-to-equity ratio is:

$$£16,000,000\ /\ £9,750,000 = 1.64$$

This means that Widget Enterprises has debts 1.64 times bigger than its assets, or that for every £1 of shares owned by the shareholders, it owes £1.64 in debt repayments. In the same way as the P/E ratio in the previous section, just knowing what one company's D/E ratio is doesn't give you much information. You need to be comparing it to similar companies in similar industries.

Some industries are very debt-heavy, just due to the nature of the work they do. This means they have higher D/E ratios in general. Aerospace companies for example often fund their activities with large amounts of debts. Physical components, engines and maintenance costs are much higher than other industries.

A high D/E ratio (mostly greater than 2) on its own isn't necessarily bad, but if it's high relative to other companies in the *same* industry, this should raise a red flag. If a company has a high D/E ratio then recurring periods of weakening profits could be a signal for financial problems and potentially even bankruptcy over the longer term. D/E ratio is also important for investors to consider because whatever the circumstances with a company's profits, they still need to meet the minimum payments on loans and other debts. The higher the D/E ratio, the higher the risk of it not being able to meet loan payments.

Looking at multiple years for a single company can also give you a sense of how they're performing over time. If the D/E ratio is increasing each year, what is it that's causing this? Are operations expanding, is the company investing in new facilities or is there something more concerning happening? Likewise, if the D/E ratio is reducing each year, this might indicate that the company is slowly improving its cash position and ability to repay its debts and as such could be a good investment.

Free-Cash-Flow per share

Free-cash-flow per share is a measure of a company's financial flexibility. This is the ability to react to unexpected expenses and investment opportunities. Ideally a company will generate more cash flow than it needs to pay the bills. When it does, the free-cash-flow per share amount will increase and strengthen its ability to pay debt, pay dividends and grow the business. It's an early indicator of the share price of the company and is often used as a guide to see if earnings will be on the increase. If they do, this will most-likely increase the share price too. It's a very good guide on how robust the business is in general.

Free-cash-flow per share is calculated by dividing the free cash flow by all of the shares being held by shareholders, otherwise known as "shares outstanding".

Free Cash Flow per share = Free Cash Flow / Number of shares outstanding

For example, let's assume Widget Enterprises Statement of Cash Flows shows operating cash flow of £200,000. It also shows capital expenditures of £100,000 for the purchase of a new building. This means Widget Enterprises has a free-cash-flow of £100,000.

Next, we find the number of shares outstanding in Widget Enterprises Annual Report to be 10,000 shares. Using this information, we know that £100,000 / 10,000 outstanding shares = £10 per share free-cash-flow. If this was more than the previous years, this shows an improving cash position and would reflect positively on the company's operations. Likewise, if cash was reducing year after year, this may worry investors and hurt the share price too as this could be a sign of lower earnings, higher costs and less efficiency.

Investors that can find companies that have high or improving free cash flow but low share prices often means the share prices will soon catch up so it might be a great time to invest. Financial analysts value free cash flow very highly.

Basic Portfolio Management

I'm intentionally keeping this section brief as new investors can go crazy trying to constantly tweak and refine their portfolios when all they really need to do is sit back and leave it alone. That being said, there are two main things you should do at regular intervals.

Short-term review of your contributions

At least once every six months but ideally no more than every 3 months, you should be reviewing your situation in terms of your investment contributions. Let me be very clear, this is *not* a review on the performance of your investments. Investing is a long-term game and the performance of your investments over a few months could be completely different to how they will perform over the long term.

This is a review of the current contributions to your investment portfolio and if they're in-line with your goals. Are you contributing too much or too little? Do you find yourself running out of money too often and therefore need to reduce the investment contributions a bit? Maybe you have more cash left over than you thought at the end of each month and so you can afford to invest some more. Things are likely to change over time as you change jobs or get promoted, especially if you work on commission, so make sure you keep these intervals fairly frequent.

Long-term review of your performance

At least once every year, you should review the performance of your investments. A bad performing investment for one year doesn't mean you should automatically sell. However, as with anything, the trajectory of companies can change and new events might mean you have access to information that could affect a company's future profitability. Do you need to act immediately? Probably not, but you need to be aware of the direction things are trending in. Do you still believe in the company and its financials? If so, sticking with it seems sensible. There will be ups and downs with absolutely *any* investment you own.

You don't need to check your portfolio's progress as much as you think you do. This might sound strange but it stops you from overreacting. Keep an eye on the news and research, but not the minute-by-minute play of your portfolios progress. Unless you can predict the future, it'll only get you flustered.

13 HINTS AND TIPS

Everyone starts somewhere and there's nothing wrong with being a newbie. I want to share with you some of the best tips I've come across as these should give you a big head start. The worry is that if you fall into any of bad traps early on, you can trick yourself into thinking *"Forget about this, investing isn't for me"* and it'll put you off completely when it shouldn't. Don't worry about making mistakes, it's inevitable that you will but hopefully you'll be able to avoid a lot of them if you know about them up front.

Active trading is a waste of money

The term "active trading" covers the buying and selling of investments over a short space of time (minutes to weeks) in order to buy at a lower price and sell at a higher price for a profit. Active trading tries to "beat the market". The stereotypical stockbroker is usually associated with this type of trading, and there are many people that do this for a living. I don't recommend this type of investing at all, especially for a beginner. I want to be clear now if I haven't been already, this book has not in any way, shape or form been written for active trading. It's not only very risky for a new investor, but any investor. Even the big, powerful institutional investors.

Trading more than necessary increases costs, as every time you trade is another cost that your gains need to offset to make it worthwhile. Short-term variation in price can't be reliably predicted and most individual investors who trade money in this way end up losing money.

Instead of actively trying to beat the market, you should only be buying and selling over the long-term. Carefully research your investments using the knowledge gained when you finish this book. You won't be getting rich overnight, but you shouldn't be getting poor overnight either.

Becoming too emotional

Financial anxiety affects people of every age and income. Finance as a topic is often seen as boring and just numbers but it's surprising how much emotions those numbers can generate. Financial anxiety is common because brits aren't taught the basics of personal finance in schools. It often means people start adult life with no real understanding of the financial skills they need to succeed. Money isn't the answer to everything, but your finances are a very real part of your overall mental and physical wellbeing.

The emotional side of investing is very real for new investors as you can quite easily get the jitters when things don't go the way you want them to. There's a lot of data out there these days which is great when you know how to use it, but it can be damaging when used incorrectly.

One of the most common traps people fall into is checking their new portfolios every 2 minutes. You've excitedly set up your first investment, nervously clicked the buy button for the first time and naturally you can't wait to see the returns of all your hard work researching the right shares, funds, bonds etc. Checking your portfolio too much can cause unnecessary panic. If you start seeing short term dips in price, you might feel compelled to do something about it like sell a particular share in a company, which could turn out to be a big mistake.

Don't just follow the herd

Just because a company is popular doesn't mean it's a good investment. Investors can get badly burned by following the masses. More popularity in a company means it gets more attention from financial analysts. It's the analyst's job to speculate on the share price of a company, and if there are more analysts speculating, there's often more attention drawn. This attention brings more speculation and more assumptions which, like a snowball effect, can generate enormous amounts of hype with a lot of people thinking they are the next big thing. Investors start piling in money, which then starts to raise the share price even more, but it's just all fluff and hype. Still, it keeps going, the share price is rising so fast which makes even more people think *"I can't miss out on this opportunity!"* until a point comes where some real news appears and shatters peoples' perceptions. As we discussed previously, the obvious examples of these are investment bubbles, but the effect doesn't have to be as obvious as that, it can be subtler.

A perfect example of this is the popular messaging app Snapchat. Snapchat's developers, Snap Inc, went public in March 2017. Their Initial Public Offering (IPO) was $17 per share. By the end of the first day this had jumped to about $26 a share. Not bad for a single day's trading, nothing too crazy. The problem was that interest in Snap shares was enormous and everyone was very excited, which meant thousands of investors flocking to throw their money at the supposed next big thing. Two months later, Snap Inc reported their earnings for the first time and it wasn't good news. They declared a $2.2 billion quarterly loss. Snap's share price fell more than 20%. The share price has slid ever since, as other big players in the industry managed to successfully copy Snapchats main features, hurting the company's growth. As of November 2018, the shares are trading for just under $6. Anyone investing at their IPO is currently sitting on a loss of about 75%. Unless Snap turns it around over the long term, it's going to be a while before anyone gets their money back, so be wary of the popular.

Make sure you look into any investment's past performance and what the experts are predicting for its performance in the future. Past performance isn't necessarily an indicator of future performance but it'll give you a good feel of the management of the company and whether their strategy is paying off in generating value for shareholders. Get to know the sector the company operates in and seek out analysts' opinions, and as above, be very wary of investing in IPOs.

Timing the market

Timing the market is when you actively try and pick the "best" time to buy a type of investment because you think it is currently about to increase in price, or sell an investment because it is about to decrease in price. It's similar to active trading. People can easily convince themselves that they're waiting for a stock to fall in price before attempting to "buy low", but the truth is, nobody can predict the precise movements of the market. It's impossible to know for certain when the market will rise or fall at any point. Even legendary investor Warren Buffett acknowledges this and was once quoted:

> *"Anything can happen at any time in markets. And no advisor, economist or TV commentator – and definitely not Charlie [Munger, Buffett's business partner] nor I – can tell you when chaos will occur. Market forecasters will fill your ear but will never fill your wallet."*

There are lots of people who claim to know how to predict the market behaviour, but this is all just smoke and mirrors. Back in 2014, various experts expected the FTSE 100 to hit a new all-time high of 8,000. This number is an index ranking figure and is derived from the weighted value of a batch of shares – the higher the value, the higher the index. The FTSE 100 started the year at 6,727. A level of 8,000 would have beat the previous all-time-highs of 6950 from December 1999. Economic forecasters at

Capital Economics said the index would reach 7,500 and analysts at Citigroup said they expected the index to reach 8,000, but it wasn't until three years later in 2017 that the FTSE 100 reached 7,500 and 8,000 still hasn't been passed. This is one example of how it's not possible for the professionals to accurately and consistently predict the market so don't even bother trying it yourself. Instead of timing the market, the "time *in* the market" is what matters – it's the length of time your investments are given to grow which is the most important factor.

Not clearing high-interest debts

Let's be realistic, debt is a reality for most families in the UK. The average UK household credit-card debt is about £7,500. If you have non-mortgage or student loan debts, and they're of the high-interest type such as typical credit card rates, rather than on 0% deals, skip back to Chapter 6 as a reminder on how to save over £7,500. Using that freed up cash to pay off your high-interest debt is hands-down one of the best investments you can make and you should absolutely start with that before even thinking about buying shares or investments. It might not be what you want to hear or why you're reading this book but it'll definitely set you on the path to creating a better life for you and your family.

If you have credit card debt and the interest-free period has expired, you're likely paying an eye-watering 19% interest rate or thereabouts. Every single pound you put towards paying off that debt is saving you 19% interest. To put it another way, in the context of investing, that's exactly the same as earning a guaranteed 19% return after taxes. It'll be hard to beat that with any investment. Any returns below your highest interest debt payments are just wiped out by the interest you're being charged on that debt. Focus on debt as the first step to building your family's wealth. This is very much your first stepping stone on the investment journey.

Don't confuse units when buying

This might seem obvious but it almost caught me out at the beginning of my investing journey! Most UK investments are listed in "GBX". This stands for Great British *Pence*. Therefore, you'll see shares for £9 listed as 900GBX. Make sure when buying investments, you enter the correct number of zeros! The denominations that investments are listed in change format depending on which stock exchange you're buying from and which provider you're using. If you end up buying a mix of US and UK shares for example, make sure you don't confuse the units on them, as shares on US exchanges are listed in USD, United States Dollars – a potentially very costly mistake!

Re-invest your dividends

Another reminder that you should always be reinvesting your dividends to maximise your returns. As we've seen in previous chapters, the difference compound interest can make is staggering, and unless you really need the money, you ought to be reinvesting everything you earn back into your investment portfolio to grow your pot quicker as the years go by. The earlier you start the more powerful the effect.

Look for hidden value

Most people know McDonalds as a fast-food chain, but what you might not know is that it's one of the world's biggest owners of land and property. McDonalds runs a franchise model, which means that about 85% of individual McDonalds around the world are mostly owned by individuals who are classed as self-employed. For the person owning the franchise – referred to as the franchisee – it's effectively running your own business but borrowing the name/brand from a bigger company.

Some of the biggest names on the high street such as KFC, Subway and Costa Coffee also use franchise models so there's nothing unique there, but what sets McDonalds apart is how they control the land that the franchises are run on. Franchisees from other businesses are usually free to pick restaurant locations as they deem suitable, but McDonalds is different. If you want to open your own McDonalds franchise, you have to lease the land/building from McDonalds HQ, which owns the land outright. The franchisee will then take on a 20-year lease, paying rent and a service fee to McDonalds HQ for the whole duration. They also pay a percentage cut of sales as is how a franchise usually works.

This is a mega earner from McDonalds because they're getting paid in multiple ways. Once from their cut of the franchise sales, another from the rent the franchisee pays to them and finally from the growing value of the land. This land is often in high-value locations. Chances are the closest McDonalds to you sits in a busy retail park or high street. These are the most visible and profitable locations for any food service to operate which is what drives the overall value of land for McDonalds HQ. Currently McDonalds has about £23 billion in global property, so don't assume that just because they serve burgers and fries that their money is based on food.

With any company, look for hidden value beyond the obvious. Not every company has a hidden gem like this, but you might be surprised if they're well-known for one thing and have big assets in other areas.

Don't Panic

The media is often sensational on movements in the major stock market indexes. Just this morning while writing this chapter, I saw emotionally-worded headlines designed to provoke reactions that talked about the FTSE 100 and how it had "plunged" by 3.2%. The US Dow Jones had "tumbled" by 3%. Tokyo's Nikkei index had "shed" a whopping…1.9%. Whilst in the grand scheme of things, these are major indexes and there's a lot of money at stake, nothing about those figures is life altering, especially for someone with a well-diversified investment portfolio. There's often talk about markets being "spooked" – whatever that means – but the point is, things are exaggerated a lot by the media and investments aren't immune to this.

With business headlines like this, it often includes financial analysts saying they're "worried" or "concerned". The job of an analyst is to set a price target on a particular share, so their opinions carry a lot of weight. An analyst's price target for a company includes assumptions of future activity, commentary on the ratios we discussed in the previous chapter and represents an expectation of the future price of the shares. There isn't a set way to calculate a price target, and different analysts use different methods with different assumptions. So, if a company is going through a bad patch – and maybe the whole industry is too – analysts will reduce their price targets. The very act of changing the price target adds fuel to the fire in extreme, or *perceived* extreme, scenarios like those "plunging" and "tumbling" indexes. This in turn makes investors react to that news and act irrationally, often at the fear of losing their money and having to act quickly, in a panic to limit any loss. It's a self-fulfilling prophecy.

The best thing about the scenarios where everything appears all doom and gloom, prices are dropping and people are panic selling is that these situations are often perfect *buying* opportunities. Investing isn't all plain sailing or logical. Long term trends where you're losing money obviously go against the aim of investing – you want to be making it not losing it – but there is a golden opportunity in short-term dips in price. Everything is effectively on sale. Many investors panic sell, often at a loss, as soon as things get uncertain. But short-term fluctuations present good buying opportunities. This is the power of pound-cost averaging, where you can buy assets cheaply when they dip in price and take advantage of their price increase later down the line. If there's any negative political or economic impact to the prices of companies that you think are still fundamentally good value, then it's time to go investment shopping.

Key Investor Information Documents (KIIDs)

Boring, but necessary. These are documents that every fund is required to have which summarises the key points of the fund in a standard format. It's tempting to skip over the small print but make sure you read these documents, you're legally obliged to if you're investing in funds. They're fact sheets that contain important information such as the overall objectives of the fund, how risky the fund is, what the charges are and the funds past performance. The standard format allows an easy comparison between funds too.

14 THE END OF THE BOOK, THE START OF YOUR JOURNEY

D epending on how much you already knew, there's been a lot to take in, so I appreciate you taking the time out of your busy schedule to read my book. As I mentioned at the beginning, I've tried to create the exact type of investing resource that I wish existed when I started out investing. This book was always meant as a starter though – it's all of the stuff I think you need to know as a bare minimum to start off well but there are plenty more resources out there. Investing is a journey towards creating a better future for you, your family and for achieving your life goals, so I hope you continue your learning with some of the resources I've listed below.

Don't stop here, research your next moves

You can find investment tips in all kinds of newspapers, websites and magazines. That's not to say all of them are good, but some will be. The hard part is separating out the good ones. I've listed a few websites that I think are good resources in this section. There are many more than this, but these are the most useful to me and I want to share that with you.

Here are several free resources I use frequently and a bit about what each focus on:

www.proactiveinvestors.co.uk - Great for updates to unknown/small-cap shares. Proactive Investors provide very good profiles on companies and the case for investing in them. They also frequently include interviews with senior company executives for further insights. Proactive Investors also has a different website version for different geographical regions so you can research internationally. They offer a good, free email newsletter.

www.monevator.com – Very knowledgeable resource for all things investing. Monevator has thorough articles that go into a lot of detail with various investing concepts and there are lots of links to more resources when you want to further your reading.

www.fool.co.uk – The Motley Fool is a site dedicated to free and subscription-based investing knowledge. They've got some very good free articles or for those willing to pay money, they offer a share advisory service. They offer a good, free email newsletter.

https://www.moneyadviceservice.org.uk/en - The Money Advice Service is one of the best resources out there for anything money or investment related. It's a government-backed resource where you can find more information about many of the concepts in this book if you want to further your reading. It also offers free, impartial money advice.

My final thoughts

What is the one thing, above all else, that you want more than anything in the world? Visualise it. Visualise having or doing that one thing you've wanted since before you can remember. Amazing feeling isn't it?

Now imagine not achieving it.

How does that make you feel? Are you disappointed? By imagining a scenario like that I certainly am.

That feeling is the drive you need to draw on to make real changes to your life. Whilst there's an almost infinite source of information out there, no guide is going to ever completely be a "paint-by-numbers" approach. It's going to take real work by you to make things happen, which includes a lot of action. Are you ready to take action?

A reminder to not be afraid if you don't have much to invest right now. I didn't when I started. Follow the money-saving tips in this book as well as many others easily available on the internet and you can free up cash much easier than you might think. Make sure you're taking advantage of concepts such as pound-cost averaging and compound interest. Just to put it into perspective, if you were to have invested the equivalent of £5 a day into a FTSE 250 index tracker fund over the past 30 years, you'd now have a pot valued at around £250,000. Investing means you have to be patient – but as you can see, the results are worth it.

Don't ignore your own expertise either. If you have any specialist knowledge of sectors or companies, you're an insider in that field and will have much more knowledge about the industry than most other people – make sure you put it to use!

Before you go, a sincere thank you for reading this book. I hope that you've enjoyed it but above all, I hope that it was useful to you. I've spent a significant amount of time writing this in the hope it helps other people starting in a similar situation to my own. A brief reminder that there is no better financial advisor for your money than you. No-one else will have the same passion to achieve your goals or the same sense of drive to improve you and your family's life as much as you do. The experience I've had on my own investing journey so far has been life changing. I'm continuing to learn every day and I hope you are too.

This may be the end of the book but it's certainly not the end of the discussion. I'd love to hear your feedback and answer any questions you have, so please contact me on theinvestordad@gmail.com. If you're on Instagram, please follow and message me "@theinvestordad" for free, regular investing knowledge and to join a family of like-minded investors. I wish you all the best as you continue your journey.

ABOUT THE AUTHOR

Dario lives with his fiancée Beth and their two children in Birmingham, England. He currently works for a FTSE100 aerospace engineering company as a team leader and has been investing alongside his day job for over 8 years. When he's not spending time with his family or researching companies, Dario enjoys gardening and Thai boxing, although not at the same time...

GLOSSARY

Active Management	Active management is the use of a human element, such as a portfolio manager, co-managers or a team of managers, to actively manage a fund's portfolio. Active managers rely on research, forecasts, and their own judgment and experience in making investment decisions on what investments to buy, hold and sell.
Active Trading	Active trading refers to buying and selling securities for quick profit based on short-term movements in price.
Asset Allocation	Asset allocation is an investment strategy that balances risk vs reward by adjusting the percentage of each asset in an investment portfolio according to the investor's own risk tolerance
Bear market	A bear market is a condition in which stock prices fall 20% or more from recent highs amid widespread pessimism and negative investor sentiment. Typically, bear markets are associated with declines in an overall market or index.
Bid-Offer spread/Bid-Ask spread	A bid-ask spread is the amount by which the ask price exceeds the bid price for an asset in the market. The bid-ask spread is essentially the difference between the highest price that a buyer is willing to pay for an asset and the lowest price that a seller is willing to accept.
Blockchain	Blockchain is a distributed, decentralized, public ledger. This is the foundational concept that makes cryptocurrency function.

Bonds	A bond is a fixed income instrument that represents a loan made by an investor to a borrower (typically a company or a government). A bond is effectively an I.O.U. between the lender and borrower that includes the details of the loan and its payments.
Bulls	A bull market is the condition of a financial market of a group of securities in which prices are rising or are expected to rise. The term "bull market" is typically reserved for extended periods in which a large portion of security prices are rising.
Capital Gains Tax (CGT)	A tax levied on profit from the sale of property or an investment
Commodities	Commodities are "hard assets" ranging from wheat to gold to oil. They are regularly traded around the world and represent some of the earliest investments that were ever made.
Common shares/stocks (also known as equity shares/stocks or ordinary shares/stocks)	Common stock is a form of corporate equity ownership. This type of share gives the stockholder the right to share in the profits of the company, and to vote on matters of corporate policy and the composition of the members of the board of directors.
Competitive advantage	Competitive advantages are conditions that allow a company or country to produce a good or service of equal value at a lower price or in a more desirable fashion. These conditions allow the productive entity to generate more sales or superior margins compared to its market rivals.
Compound Interest	Compound interest (or compounding interest) is interest calculated on the initial principal, which also includes all of the accumulated interest of previous periods of a deposit or loan.

Consumer Price Index (CPI)	The CPI is a measure that examines the weighted average of prices of a basket of consumer goods and services, such as transportation, food and medical care.
Consumer Price Index including Housing (CPIH)	CPIH is similar to CPI and is a new measure of the annual rate of UK consumer price inflation that includes owner occupiers' housing costs.
Contracts for Difference (CFD)	A CFD is a popular form of derivative trading. CFD trading enables you to speculate on the rising or falling prices of fast-moving global financial markets, such as forex, indices, commodities, shares and treasuries.
Cryptocurrency	A cryptocurrency is a digital asset designed to work as a medium of exchange that uses strong cryptography to secure financial transactions, control the creation of additional units, and verify the transfer of assets
Debt crowdfunding	Debt based crowdfunding encompasses several different types of crowd-based lending. These include mini-bonds and peer-to-peer lending (sometimes known as 'peer-2-peer' or 'P2P' lending). Essentially, a large amount of retail investors (the crowd) lend money through a platform to a business or individual.
Debt-to-Equity Ratio (D/E)	The D/E ratio is an important metric used in corporate finance. It is a measure of the degree to which a company is financing its operations through debt versus wholly owned funds. More specifically, it reflects the ability of shareholder equity to cover all outstanding debts in the event of a business downturn.
Defaulting	In finance, default is failure to meet the legal obligations (or conditions) of a loan and loan payments.

Direct Debit	An arrangement made with a bank that allows a third party to transfer money from a person's account on agreed dates, typically in order to pay bills
Diversification	Diversification is a risk management strategy that mixes a wide variety of investments within a portfolio. The rationale behind this technique is that a portfolio constructed of different kinds of assets will, on average, yield higher long-term returns and lower the risk of any individual holding.
Dividend	A dividend is a payment made by a corporation to its shareholders, usually as a distribution of profits.
Dividend Pay-out Ratio	The dividend pay-out ratio is the number of dividends paid to stockholders relative to the amount of total net income of a company
Dividend Tax	A tax levied on dividend payments. For the UK, this is currently 7.5% if you're in the basic rate tax band.
Dividend Yield	The dividend yield is the ratio of a company's annual dividend compared to its share price. The dividend yield is an estimate of the dividend-only return of a stock investment.
Equity Crowdfunding	Equity crowdfunding is the process whereby people (the 'crowd') invest in an early-stage unlisted company (a company that is not listed on a stock market) in exchange for shares in that company.
Exchange Traded Fund (ETF)	An exchange-traded fund (ETF) is an investment fund traded on stock exchanges, much like stocks. An ETF holds assets such as stocks, commodities, or bonds.
Foreign Exchange (FX) Costs	The costs associated with exchanging money from one currency to another.

Free-cash-flow per share	Free cash flow per share is determined by dividing free cash flow by the total number of shares outstanding. This serves as a measurement of a change in earnings per share, which is a metric that is used to assess the financial health of a business.
Full Replication	This is how a market is represented in an index tracker fund. Full replication has a fund which holds the same percentage of shares in a company as they represent in the index that is being tracked.
Fund	A fund pools together the money of lots of different investors, and a fund manager invests on their behalf. Funds can invest in various types of asset, such as shares, bonds or property, depending on the investment objective of the fund.
Fund accumulation units	An accumulation unit is a kind of investment in which the income is not paid out as cash to the investor and is instead reinvested into the fund directly.
Fund income units	An income unit is a kind of investment in which the income is paid out as cash to the investor.
GBX	Great British Pence, the currency denomination that is used on the London Stock Exchange.
Gilts	A gilt is a bond denominated in British pounds issued by the treasury, and payments on gilts are backed by the credit of the U.K. government.
Inflation	A general increase in prices and fall in the purchasing value of money.
Initial Coin Offering (ICO)	An ICO is the cryptocurrency space's rough equivalent to an IPO in the mainstream investment world. ICOs act as fundraisers of sorts; a company looking to create a new coin, app, or service launches an ICO.

Interest Tax	Tax levied on interest payments.
Key Investor Information Documents (KIIDs)	KIIDs are regulatory documents produced by fund managers about funds.
Large-cap	Large-cap stocks refer to firms which have a market capitalisation of more than $10 billion.
Mid-Cap	Mid-cap stocks refer to firms which have a market capitalisation of more than $2 billion and less than $10 billion.
Open Ended Investment Company (OEIC)	An OEIC is a collective investment vehicle that pools your money with other investors.
Partial Replication	This is how a market is represented in an index tracker fund. Partial replication holds a proportion of the underlying index but due to complexity or cost, does not hold every single part of the index. It is the opposite to Full Replication
Passive management	Passive management is a style of management associated with funds and ETFs where a fund's portfolio mirrors a market index. Passive management is the opposite of active management in which a fund's manager attempts to beat the market with various investing strategies and buying/selling decisions of a portfolio's assets.
Pound-cost averaging	Investing a sum of money over a period of time, rather than all at once, is known as pound-cost averaging. The idea behind pound-cost averaging is to provide some protection in case the market drops shortly after the money is invested. Instead of the entire investment losing value, only the invested portion does, and the benefit is that the remainder is then invested at lower prices.

Preferred Shares	A share which entitles the holder to a fixed dividend, whose payment takes priority over that of ordinary share dividends. Preferred shares usually do not give shareholders voting rights.
Price-to-Earnings Ratio (P/E)	The price-to-earnings ratio indicates the dollar amount an investor can expect to invest in a company in order to receive one dollar of that company's earnings.
Real Estate Investment Trust (REIT)	REITs are companies that own or finance income-producing real estate in a range of property sectors.
Retail Price Index (RPI)	RPI is one of the two main measures of consumer inflation produced by the United Kingdom's Office for National Statistics.
Robo-Advisor	Robo-advisors are a class of financial adviser that provide advice or investment management online with minimal human intervention. They provide digital financial advice based on mathematical rules or algorithms.
Savings Chatbot	Similar to robo-advisors but focused purely on savings. These are apps or services that automatically save money based on mathematical rules or algorithms with minimal human intervention.
Shareholder/stockholder	A shareholder is an individual or a business that legally owns one or more shares of stock in a public or private business.
Shares/stocks/equities	Shares are the units of the ownership of a company, usually traded on the stock market. A person that owns shares is a shareholder.
Small-Cap	Small-cap stocks refer to firms which have a market capitalisation of more than $300 million and less than about $2 billion.

Stock exchange	A stock exchange is a facility where stock brokers and traders can buy and sell investments, such as shares of stock and bonds and other financial instruments.
Stock market	The stock market refers to the entire collection of markets and exchanges where regular activities of buying, selling and issuance of shares of publicly-held companies take place.
Stock market index	A stock index or stock market index is a measurement of a section of the stock market. It is computed from the prices of selected stocks.
Trading Margin	Buying "on margin" is borrowing money from a stockbroker to buy stock. You can think of it as a loan from your brokerage. Margin trading allows you to buy more stock than you'd be able to normally.
Transaction Costs	The costs associated with buying and selling investments, usually charged by the stockbroker in the form of a commission per transaction.
Unit Trust	An OEIC is a collective investment vehicle that pools your money with other investors. It is very similar to an OEIC.
Withholding Tax	A tax deducted at source, it is usually levied by some countries on interest or dividends paid to a person resident outside that country.
Active Management	Active management is the use of a human element, such as a portfolio manager, co-managers or a team of managers, to actively manage a fund's portfolio. Active managers rely on research, forecasts, and their own judgment and experience in making investment decisions on what investments to buy, hold and sell.

Active Trading	Active trading refers to buying and selling securities for quick profit based on short-term movements in price.
Asset Allocation	Asset allocation is an investment strategy that balances risk vs reward by adjusting the percentage of each asset in an investment portfolio according to the investor's own risk tolerance
Bear market	A bear market is a condition in which stock prices fall 20% or more from recent highs amid widespread pessimism and negative investor sentiment. Typically, bear markets are associated with declines in an overall market or index.
Bid-Offer spread/Bid-Ask spread	A bid-ask spread is the amount by which the ask price exceeds the bid price for an asset in the market. The bid-ask spread is essentially the difference between the highest price that a buyer is willing to pay for an asset and the lowest price that a seller is willing to accept.
Blockchain	Blockchain is a distributed, decentralized, public ledger. This is the foundational concept that makes cryptocurrency function.
Bonds	A bond is a fixed income instrument that represents a loan made by an investor to a borrower (typically a company or a government). A bond is effectively an I.O.U. between the lender and borrower that includes the details of the loan and its payments.
Bulls	A bull market is the condition of a financial market of a group of securities in which prices are rising or are expected to rise. The term "bull market" is typically reserved for extended periods in which a large portion of security prices are rising.
Capital Gains Tax (CGT)	A tax levied on profit from the sale of property or an investment.

Commodities	Commodities are "hard assets" ranging from wheat to gold to oil. They are regularly traded around the world and represent some of the earliest investments that were ever made.
Common shares/stocks (also known as equity shares/stocks or ordinary shares/stocks)	Common stock is a form of corporate equity ownership. This type of share gives the stockholder the right to share in the profits of the company, and to vote on matters of corporate policy and the composition of the members of the board of directors.
Competitive advantage	Competitive advantages are conditions that allow a company or country to produce a good or service of equal value at a lower price or in a more desirable fashion. These conditions allow the productive entity to generate more sales or superior margins compared to its market rivals.

Printed in Great Britain
by Amazon